REVIEW

In this splendid book, Melinda Powell eloquently describes using her dreams for spiritual insight, healing, and exploring the 'stirrings of her soul' in her quest for wholeness. Her courageous process of actively surrendering in dream lucidity brings her experiences that are deeply moving and awe-inspiring. She highlights how her dreams connect to esoteric spiritual traditions and modern physics, while extending Carl Jung's alchemical model to encompass transformative lucid dreaming. Importantly, she also shows how dream lucidity can enhance waking life — including service to others. Her experiences in dreams involving light, mirrors and wormholes are evocative of a future in which explorations of consciousness and physical reality go hand in hand — for a true bridging of spirit and science. I hope that her book will be required reading for future generations of physicists. I feel sure that readers will enjoy it immensely and that it will aid them in their journey 'beyond the limitations of time and space to Spirit'.

Don Middendorf
Professor Emeritus of Physics and Consciousness Studies,
The Evergreen State College, Olympia, WA

ಽ ❊ ಐ

Melinda Powell invites us to surrender to the Black Light of lucid dreaming to discover the 'soul medicine' to heal and awaken. Based on her own experience of lucid dreaming, Powell relays her journey of personal growth, a growth that catalyses the soul's essence anew. Excerpts from her dream journal allow the reader to follow her inward journey home in ways that will inspire them to explore how the Black Light may be uniquely revealed in their own dreams.

Rosemarie Anderson, PhD
Author of *The Divine Feminine Tao Te Ching*

ℰ ❄ ℛ

The path of Lucid Surrender unveils a radically new approach to exploring the realm of lucid dreaming. With ever increasing levels of trust and acceptance, Melinda Powell opens herself to following the winds of her inner awareness to discover what it wishes her to experience. This book encourages lucid dreamers to 'let go,' accepting what comes with a grateful heart to lovingly engage their deeper wisdom and multi-dimensionality. A must read for those who seek a direct encounter with the eternal part of their being-ness.

Robert Waggoner
Author of *Lucid Dreaming: Gateway to the Inner Self*,
and co-author of *Lucid Dreaming Plain and Simple*

ℰ ❄ ℛ

With *Lucid Surrender*, Melinda Powell makes another valuable contribution to the field of transpersonal psychology and, more widely, to humanity. The author applies her professional experience as a psychotherapist, and her own profound capacity for transpersonal dreaming, to Carl Jung's process of Individuation. Drawing on alchemical symbolism, she invites the reader into her visions, embodied dreams and psycho-spiritual journey, going beyond Carl Jung's alchemical model to make readily accessible the subtle and ineffable. Through this well-researched and lucid text, the author's unique window on the world of the unconscious and the power of Lucid Surrender offers the reader a practical therapeutic guide for decoding the Transpersonal, bringing the dreamer to a deeply felt sense of what it can mean to realise one's soul desire.

Diane Greig, Ph.D.,
Founder of the Pacific Northwest Dream Community, Canada
Creator / Host of *Invisible Women*: The Podcast

ℬ ❄ ℛ

This important work re-visions the widely misunderstood mystical topic of 'Black Light', a phenomenon described by mystics such as St. John of the Cross. Although light is not normally connected with darkness in this way, Black Light as understood by Melinda Powell is distinct in possessing a vibrant luminosity. The author, as both psychotherapist and dream guide, draws on examples from her own extraordinary capacity for dream lucidity to show how the experience of Black Light in lucid dreams can trigger a transcending of normal dream 'reality'. Through a process that Melinda Powell calls 'Lucid Surrender', she reveals how immersion in the Light of pure Spirit can lead to profound spiritual awakening.

Nigel Hamilton, PhD
Director, Centre for Counselling and Psychotherapy Education, London
Co-Founder of the Dream Research Institute, London and author of
Awakening Through Dreams: The Journey Through the Inner Landscape

☼ ✤ ☾

Lucid Surrender

*The Alchemy of the Soul
in Lucid Dreaming*

Lucid Surrender

*The Alchemy of the Soul
in Lucid Dreaming*

Melinda Powell

First published in the United Kingdom by
Archive Publishing
Shaftesbury, Dorset, England

www.archivepublishing.co.uk

Designed at Archive Publishing by Ian Thorp MA
Printed and bound in England by CMP (UK) Ltd., Poole, Dorset.

10 9 8 7 6 5 4 3 2 1

Copyright © 2021 Archive Publishing
Text Copyright © Melinda Powell, 2021

Melinda Powell asserts the moral right to be
identified as the author of this work in accordance with the
Copyright, Design and Patents Act, 1988.

The term Lucid Surrender ™ is a registered trademark of Melinda Powell.

This book is copyright under the Berne Convention.
No reproduction without the prior permission of the publisher.
All rights reserved.

A CIP catalogue record for this book is available from The British Library.

ISBN 978-1-906289-52-2 (Paperback)

Cover design & Parts I-IV title page artwork © Eri Griffin Illustrations.

*The author and publisher shall have no liability or responsibility
to any person or entity regarding any loss, damage or injury incurred,
or alleged to have incurred, directly or indirectly, by the information
contained in this book.*

Dedication

To the Spirit that moves through dreams
and awakens our hearts to Love

*...in this surrender of the soul's gift,
the soul loves again as if for the first time.* [1]
— St John of the Cross

Contents

List of Illustrations		xiii
Foreword by Stanton Marlan, Ph.D., ABPP		xv
Acknowledgements		xvii
Author's Introduction		xxi

Part I   Awakening the Heart to Lucid Surrender

1	Lucid Surrender and the Holy Tree: An Illustration	3
2	Lucid Dreaming and Lucid Surrender	7
3	On Lucid Surrender: A Path to Lucidity	19
4	Healing Dreams in Lucidity	33

Part II   Awake In Sleep! Lucid Dream Alchemy

5	The Alchemist's Study: Lucid Dream Alchemy	45
6	The Fullness of the Void: Black Light in Lucid Surrender	61
7	The Spiritual Alchemy of Light within Darkness	79
8	Lucid Surrender and the Alchemical *Coniunctio*: A Post-Jungian Approach	97

Part III   The Mirror of the Heart

9	The Spiritual Science of Mirrors	123
10	The Mirror and the Snake: Personal Reflections on the Waking Dream	135
11	Through the Looking Glass in Lucidity	143
12	Wormholes in the Lucid Void	157

Part IV   *Light, Love and Laughter in Lucid Surrender*

13	Moving from Conditioned Reality to Freedom of Heart	175
14	The Gentle Humour of Lucidity	189
15	The Sacred Sands of Lucid Surrender	197
16	Becoming an Astronomer of Dreams	205

Epilogue	213
Appendix: Guidance on the Path of Lucid Surrender	215
Bibliography	223
About the Author	235
Credits	237

xiii

List of Illustrations

Part I	The Tree of Life	xxviii
Part II	The Black Sun	42
Part III	Through the Mirror	120
Part IV	Celestial Dream Tigers	172

The primary source for the following figures can be found in the main text. Numbering and titles have been given here for ease of reference.

Figure	Title	Page
1.	The Alchemist's Study	46
2.	*Dormiens Vigila*	47
3.	*Tai Ji* (*Yin* and *Yang*)	48
4.	The Ouroboros	53
5.	The Four-Fold Spheres	54
6.	The *Sol Niger* of *Nigredo*	67
7.	The *Nigredo* Standing on the *Rotundum*	73
8.	The Alchemical Flask — *Nigredo*	83
9.	The Alchemical Flask — *Albedo*	84
10.	The Alchemical Flask — *Citrinitas*	88
11.	The Alchemical Flask — *Rubedo*	92
12.	The Alchemical Fountain	101
13.	The King and Queen	102
14.	*Sol* and *Luna*	104

15.	The Alchemical Bath	105
16.	Ecstatic Union	106
17.	The Hermaphrodite on the Sepulchre	107
18.	The Soul Ascends	108
19.	Divine Dew of *Albedo*	108
20.	The Soul Returns	108
21.	Resurrected Hermaphrodite & the Moon Tree	110
22.	The Winged Royal Couple	111
23.	The Winged Sun	111
24.	The Winged Hermaphrodite on the Sepulchre	112
25.	Wisdom Ascends	112
26.	Divine Dew of *Citrinitas*	113
27.	Wisdom Returns	113
28.	The Resurrected Hermaphrodite and Sun Tree	115
29.	The Risen Christ	116

Foreword

In Melinda Powell's new book on lucid dreaming, she continues to make creative contributions to understanding the mystery of dreams. Lucid dreaming has been a bit of an enigma that has in recent times been given more scientific attention. Melinda takes into account current scientific studies, including the growing literature and findings of the American Psychological Association. In addition to the scientific literature, she is well aware of the long-term recognition and value given to lucid dreaming in a number of depth psychological and spiritual traditions, including the practice of Tibetan dream yoga. Although resonant with Jungian, alchemical, transpersonal and other perspectives, she offers her own individual insights and discoveries into the world of lucid dreaming.

Lucid dreaming has been described as entering into the experience of a dream while feeling oneself to be conscious within it. Courageously, Melinda explores her own lucid dreams by releasing her 'ego will' — what she comes to call 'Lucid Surrender', a process through which she progressively enters into the Black Light and dark illumination of her dreams. The result of this release leads to an experience parallel with what the alchemists referred to as the *lumen naturae*, the light of nature or the light of darkness itself — a primordial phenomenon that links light and darkness into what Jung called a *coniunctio oppositorum*, or unity of opposites.

For Melinda, 'Lucid Surrender' and moving beyond

binaries open a pathway into the depths of the soul, an alchemical-like and poetic descent, a spiritual journey through which she explores the mercurial wisdom of dreams and advances new ideas that have both personal and archetypal relevance. With remarkable hermetic discipline, Melinda captures and shares her dream experiences and personal life in a way that gives substance to her insights. A remarkable aspect of Melinda's work is the positivity she discovers in her research: the fullness of the void, the awakening and freedom of the heart, and the healing, holiness and illumination she finds in her dreams.

In my own work on the alchemical black sun, I have noted similar experiences of positivity, but have also encountered the darkest aspects of suffering, despair, and hopelessness. What I find so valuable and resonant in Melinda's work is her recognition that by entering deeply into this darkness rather than turning away from it, one can discover the light within the darkness itself. Melinda's emphasis on 'Lucid Surrender' into this darkness is a wonderful contribution to understanding the mysterious depths of dreaming, lucidity, and life itself. Lucidity signifies being suffused with light — glowing, effulgent, bright, translucent and clear. Such statements are a fitting description for Melinda's contribution and this new book is a gift to all those interested in the mysteries of dreaming, the depths of psychological and spiritual life, and the process of soul making.

Stanton Marlan, Ph.D., ABPP
Jungian analyst and author of *The Black Sun: The Alchemy and Art of Darkness* and *C.G. Jung and the Alchemical Imagination: Passages into the Mysteries of Psyche and Soul*

Acknowledgements

As I write, early on this dark and still winter's morning, a candle burns. Outside, the sheen of frost covers the ground like moonlight while, asleep in their beds, people dream.

Looking back over the year when I began this book at the start of the Covid-19 pandemic in 2020, it feels as if not only I but all of humanity — the whole planet indeed — has been struggling to give birth to new life. In the face of so much illness, loss and death, I am grateful simply to be alive and well and afforded this opportunity to write during such strange and troubled times.

Once, in a lucid dream, I was speaking with a young man about the nature of Soul. Suddenly the scene changed to a desolate city street. 'Hey,' I remarked, 'this is a dream, so tell me what happened to Soul!' He turned towards me, shrugged, and said, 'Sometimes it has to be like that; it's part of the process. It can't always be spring.' And yet, we know, someday, spring will come.

Meanwhile, we each offer up what we can. For myself, this book is my devotional on the life-giving love that comes alive in open hearts, loving hands and dreams, a sacrifice-of-praise to the Spirit for whom, as the Psalmist reminds us, 'darkness is as light.'

In *Lucid Surrender*, I have been blessed to see the Lord in many beautiful forms. I am humbly indebted to the Spirit and all the Holy Beings for their patience with me over many dreams as I have learned to become more trusting. I am also grateful to the Sunday school teachers of my childhood, Mrs Preston and Mrs Yankowski, who taught me that even prophets like Moses, upon whom God shone His face, had their doubts. Nevertheless, Moses got on with the job at hand! So the least I can do is to recollect and share my experience of Lucid Surrender, keeping faith with the guidance of my dreams.

Among those who have helped me, first and foremost I offer my eternal thanks to my dear husband Andrew, whose editorial skills have lovingly helped me to forge what the soul knows into living words.

I also thank artist Eri Griffin, whose stunning talent brings the Beauty and Truth in darkness to light.

When I first dreamed of luminous Black Light, given my religious and cultural preconceptions, I feared that this might herald the presence of evil. When I told my brother Carey about this, he replied, 'Oh you with your visions! All I ever dream about is being stuck in a shopping mall! I am sure that God is big enough to hold your dreams.' I was glad to be reassured. I thank Carey and my eldest brother, Steve, for their steadfast love.

A few years on, I had another crisis of doubt about the Black Light when, in a dream, it appeared to radiate from a Black Sun (I share this dream in Chapter Six). Some years after, I discovered a ground-breaking book, *The Black Sun: The Alchemy and Art of Darkness*, by Stanton Marlan. I am grateful to have come across the fruits of the author's research on the Black Sun, both in theory and in practice as a psychologist, and for his profound understanding of mystical

Divine Darkness. The book encouraged me to trust the Black Light and thence to allow the lucid dreams to unfold. It is a great honour that Stanton Marlan has written the foreword to this book.

Here, too, my indebtedness to Carl Jung for his dedication to Psyche and his fearless exploration of the Soul's depths and love's alchemy. When I first wrote an article on dream lucidity and Jung's alchemical model, I wondered, 'How can I describe Lucid Surrender from a Jungian perspective?' That night, I dreamed that Jung sat down opposite me in an old-fashioned easy chair, smoking his pipe and peering at me through his spectacles. Startled, I thought to myself, 'Well, here's Jung himself. He'll help me!' We talked for some time about his own lucid dreams, surrender, and the mysterious union of opposites in alchemy. When I woke up, I made good progress on the writing!

Three years before I began writing this book, fellow lucid dreamer Robert Waggoner appeared in a dream and said to me, 'You have a truly unique contribution to bring to the dreams, and I wish you would get it out there in published form.' Thank you to Robert and many others for giving me numerous opportunities to write and speak about Lucid Surrender, and for spurring me on to finish this book.

In this regard, I owe much to the International Association for the Studies of Dreams for providing a safe and inspiring space in which to share and explore dreams, dreamwork and dream research with so many friends and colleagues around the world, especially Diane Greig, a kindred spirit.

Closer to home, my heartfelt thanks to my dear friend

Sarah Young, who has shared in the realisation of so many dreams with me and so carefully read this manuscript.

I would particularly like to thank Nigel Hamilton, a physicist, psychotherapist, Sufi teacher, and founder of the Centre for Counselling and Psychotherapy (CCPE) in London, where I trained in psychotherapy and transpersonal dreamwork. There, in my advanced training, I was first introduced to the treasure trove of Islamic esotericism found in the teachings of Ibn Arabi and his modern interpreters, especially Henry Corbin.

At CCPE, Nigel and I shared many ideas about dreams, and so we went on to co-found the Dream Research Institute, which has provided wonderful opportunities for enlarging our collective understanding and appreciation of dreams. I am happy to know that the Institute continues under the direction of Dave Billington.

Not least, I would like to thank Ian Thorp of Archive Publishing for the care and attention he has bestowed on the production of this volume.

As this morning's candle burns low, I will end by giving thanks for the mystery of Light that shines upon us and the mystery of Night that guides us to Love.

Author's Introduction

Now in dreams one conquers, walks, or flies simultaneously, and the imagination has room for it all; but how shall mere speech find room for it? [2]

— Synesius of Cyrene (Bishop of Ptolemais, 5th century)

At the outset, I need to say that I see my dreams as belonging to everyone — as much to you as they do to me. I hope they speak to your innermost heart, lift your spirits and help you to know that you are not alone, that you are loved, and part of Creation, more wondrous than we can imagine. Dreams impart a universal message, encouraging each of us to trust in life and in the love that surrounds us all every moment, even beyond death.

I have been told many times, in waking life and when dreaming, to 'share the dreams'. One time, when I was told as much in a dream, I wondered aloud in the dream why anyone would listen to someone who happened to grow up on a suburban street in Orange, California. 'Why me?' I asked. In response, I was simply told, 'You know the dreams are to be shared.' And so I have.

In childhood, I was fortunate to spend a good deal of time in nature, exploring the foothills, deserts, mountains and beaches of my homeland. My interest in dreams stems from my early years when I first learned about the biblical visions of Joseph and Daniel. As a child, I intuitively desired to work in the ministry of the Spirit. In my teens, whenever I felt depressed, I searched the Bible for every reference to the Holy Spirit I could find, thus becoming acquainted with a wonderful healing Presence that I came to recognise in my dreams.

Through becoming more attentive to the expression of Spirit in daily life, my depression lifted. As an adult, I considered studying theology before deciding on English literature and completing a Master's in the subject. During that time, a professor teaching on the course introduced me to my first book on dreams (apart from the Bible), by John Sanford, Episcopal priest and Jungian analyst. The title was *Dreams: God's Forgotten Language*. I ended up writing to Sanford and sharing a dream with him. He replied that the dream was inviting me to work on the subject of dreams and to write. It took many years before I would do so, but in the meantime, I began to pay more attention to my dreams, recording them and reflecting on them.

In 1990, following dream guidance, I volunteered with the United States Peace Corps as a Teacher Trainer in Eastern Europe. I viewed the work ahead as spiritual service that could contribute to life behind the newly fallen Iron Curtain. In Poland, I coordinated the English Department of a three-year Teacher Training College in the town of Torun, described as 'the Gothic pearl of Poland'. There, I married, and since then, Europe has been my home. Over the past twenty years, my travels, work and studies in literature, comparative religion and psychology, along with all that I have learned from my life relationships, have helped me build up a better understanding of myself, the world, dreams and the Divine.

After living and working in Poland and Switzerland for several years, in 2000 my Polish husband and I moved to London, where I continued with post-graduate studies in Psychology and Religion while working as a research associate at Heythrop, an interfaith Jesuit College.

In 2001, my mother died. During my bereavement, I had a number of dreams that led me to train in psychotherapy at the Centre for Counselling and Psychotherapy Education. There, I learned to work with my own dreams and those of others in a therapeutic context.

The Centre proved to be the right place for me as its Director, Nigel Hamilton, specialised in dreams as a vehicle for spiritual transformation. Having completed my training, in 2009 I was appointed Director of the charitable organisation Help Counselling, in London, which I ran for seven years. In 2012, Nigel Hamilton and I co-founded the Dream Research Institute, which I subsequently directed for seven years as well.

This marked a time of intense professional work, along with major upheavals in my personal life, including divorce. In 2016, I was blessed to marry again, and in the fulfilment of a new life with my husband Andrew, I could at last settle down to more writing. Serendipitously, at the beginning of 2019, I was commissioned to write a book on dreams. I felt a strong sense of urgency to finish the book in the space of one year. A number of dreams had pressed this upon me. I recall one dream in which 'Bob Dylan' appeared and told me, 'It's time to come away with me now. You're getting older now and there isn't a lot of time left!'

When I sat down to write my first book, *The Hidden Lives*

of Dreams, I had no idea that a global pandemic would be sweeping the planet just when the book was due to be published the following year. In such circumstances, no official book launch could take place. But the book went out into the world nonetheless, hopefully to plant seeds of encouragement in those who read it, especially in such nightmarish times.

Under the 'lockdowns' of the coronavirus pandemic in 2020, I used the time to peruse my writings of the previous decade that had been specifically concerned with the practice of 'Lucid Surrender', a spiritual path of soul awakening shown to me by my lucid dreams. Alongside my journal entries detailing hundreds of lucid surrender dreams, I reviewed the various presentations and workshops given, in addition to magazine articles and book chapters I had written.

I am deeply grateful to my beloved husband Andrew for helping to make the writing of both *The Hidden Lives of Dreams* and this book possible, and for his tireless editing of the manuscript. As the pandemic spread globally, he and I went into what we called 'protective seclusion' to shield ourselves from the contagion as it moved in waves across the UK and the world. Instead of going out into the world to volunteer, as I have done before, I undertook volunteer counselling from home on the phone and online while continuing to write.

I have divided this book into four parts, organised thematically rather than chronologically. Part One serves as an introduction to Lucid Surrender. Part Two draws on alchemical teachings and the alchemical model of Carl Jung as a way to convey the qualities of light, particularly Black Light, in Lucid Surrender. I should add that I have chosen alchemical imagery because in bypassing the literality of the spoken word in its expression of Soul, it has remained free of the dogmatic assertions that many people hold about religion. Part Three takes the reader into the perception of dreams as mirrors, reflecting not only our personal psychology but also as thresholds to other dimensions of Being. Part Four guides the dreamer deeper still into the joy, light and love of lucidity as a sacred endeavour. This work draws primarily on my own learning from the practice of Lucid Surrender. Readers seeking more knowledge of the essentials of dreaming, secondary sources and research in the field of sleep and dreams will find an extensive bibliography in *The Hidden Lives of Dreams*, which serves as a prelude to this work.

I mentioned earlier that I had been guided to undertake training in transpersonal psychotherapy. For the reader unfamiliar with this approach, it may be helpful briefly to outline how the transpersonal perspective has been pivotal in my exploration of Lucid Surrender.

The core of transpersonal psychology relates to life's Big Questions: What gives our lives meaning? How do we express the Highest Good or Divine in our lives? How do we live fully? We find these questions asked and answered in our dreams. From the transpersonal viewpoint, dreams open the psyche to the profoundly sacred and divine qualities found in the depths of the unconscious. In this way, dreams are able to facilitate inner transformation. This has great significance for well-being because, as Carl Jung claimed, it is the encounter with the numinous, with a powerful healing Presence, that is the 'real therapy'.[3]

Each of us has the potential to discover this 'real therapy' for ourselves when we learn to 'wake up in sleep' by becoming lucid, meaning that we become aware that we dream while we are actually dreaming. In lucid dreams, we can choose the action we take in the dream state, much as we do in the waking world. If we choose consciously to align our individual will with the 'Highest Will'[4] and to surrender to the awareness that we 'belong to more than ourselves',[5] irrepressible new experiences of being and knowing arise. These involve transformative numinous encounters that empower us to enact creative change in the waking world. I have named this practice 'Lucid Surrender'. The call to 'wake up' to a greater wisdom and deeper love echoes throughout the Wisdom Traditions. The more we 'wake up' to our dreams, the more we wake up to life. And that's something no one should miss!

In compiling this material and reflecting on my own understanding of Lucid Surrender over time, I am reminded of a quote from one of the early Church Fathers, Synesius of Cyrene, who wrote, 'It is no mean achievement to pass on to another something of a strange nature that has stirred in one's own soul.'[6] The reader so inclined will understand that I have done my best to share what my soul has known and to communicate the power, grace, mercy, knowing, ecstasy and love of Lucid Surrender. Words both reveal and conceal, illumine and veil. Therefore, let our dreams speak for themselves. At the heart of each dream, a sacred space, a *temenos*, awaits. May each of us find our way into Lucid Surrender, in a spirit of gratitude and humility, clothed in grace.

NOTES:

1. See *St John of the Cross (San Juan de la Cruz): Alchemist of the Soul: His Life, His Poetry, His Prose*, trans. and with commentary by Antonio T. de Nicolás (York Beach, Maine: Samuel Weisser, Inc., 1989), 235.
2. From *Concerning Dreams*, cited by Morton T. Kelsey in his *God, Dreams, and Revelations: A Christian Interpretation of Dreams* (Minneapolis, MI: Augsburg Fortress Publishing, 1991), 252.
3. Carl Gustav Jung, the founder of Analytical Psychology, as cited in *C.G. Jung: Word and Image*, ed. Aniela Jaffé, Bollingen Series XCVII, Vol. 2 (Princeton, NJ: Princeton University Press, 1979), 123.
4. In his book, *The Act of Will*, Roberto Assagioli, founder of Psychosynthesis, describes the 'highest will', which gives us the capacity to act with compassion towards ourselves, others and all of creation. (New York, NY: Penguin Group, 1973), 106–122. The expression 'Highest Will' also appears in original work of Rabbi Azriel of Gerona Spain, 1160-1238 C.E., as translated into English by Aryeh Kaplan in his book, *Meditation and Kabbalah* (Lanham, Maryland: Rowman & Littlefield, Inc., 1995), 121.
5. A quote from Andrew Powell's *The Ways of the Soul: A Psychiatrist Reflects, Essays on Life, Death and Beyond* (London: Muswell Hill Press, 2017), xvii.
6. Synesisus of Cyrene, *On Dreams*, ed. and trans. Augustine Fitzgerald, *The Essays and Hymns of Synesius of Cyrene*, Vols. 1–2 (Oxford: Oxford University Press, 1930), as cited in *The Secret History of Dreams* by Robert Moss (Novato, California: New World Library, 2009), 69.

The Tree of Life

Part 1

Awakening the Heart to Lucid Surrender

I sleep, but my heart wakes.

— Song of Solomon 5:2

Chapter 1

LUCID SURRENDER AND THE HOLY TREE: AN ILLUSTRATION [7]

Beloved gaze in thine own heart
The Holy tree is growing there... [8]

— William Butler Yeats

The call to the heart in Lucid Surrender echoes the poet's plea to his beloved to gaze into her own heart and look upon the Holy Tree growing there. Like the roots of a well-established tree, Lucid Surrender extends into our earthiness, our physical body at rest in sleep, quiet in the night. With the onrush of lucidity, we are carried into the darkness of the void, deeper into our hearts, until our consciousness branches out, becoming ever finer and more subtle, suffused with light — 'the changing colour of its fruit' — as new life is born in the waking world through the breath of the Spirit.

I invite you now to gaze into your own heart, to stand before the Holy Tree that grows there, to still your mind, focus on a holy name or sacred song, and for us to share in a Lucid Surrender dream of mine, one that I have called 'The Tree of Life', as if it were your own:

With lucidity, I bow my head, and, suddenly, my soul feels free of my physical body and lifts onto the Black Light! My invisible arms open to the cool winds as if I were a kite stretched across the sky. But then an unseen Being reaches from behind me, pushing my invisible hands together ever so gently, palm to palm, as they would appear in prayer. I feel the Being's gentleness and intelligence and say 'Thank you' for this reminder of where I need to bring my focus: I begin to sing a sacred song. Delight dances delicately around and through me. In the illumined blackness, I cry out: 'I know you Holy Beings are there.' With this, tiny specks of glittering light surround me, each speck holding a Being of light as they move like flocks of starlings across the black.

The movement finally stops and before me, spread across an infinite expanse of shining darkness, there emerge concentric rings of intense red. A desire to immerse myself in the red takes hold, and I wonder if the colour green will appear next. Instead, bands of rich purple fill the outer rings. 'Red and purple,' I think to myself. 'These are the colours of royalty: This is the Divine!' But, rather than staying focused on the wondrous feelings aroused by the light form, my thoughts turn towards what will happen next.

I know from previous lucid dreams that when I start thinking about what is happening, my concentration often breaks, thus ending the dream, while if I can focus on the profound feelings present, the lucid dream will continue. As I struggle to focus my mind by singing a sacred song and breathing deeply, from the centre of the concentric rings there emerges a branching tree of red. 'The Tree of Life!' I exclaim inwardly. The boughs rise up and reach out to include me in their embrace, as I am lifted up on the red, leafy branches and the blackness into another dream.

At the heart of Lucid Surrender, we gaze into our own hearts, and become one with the light of the Holy Tree growing there. With our bodies rooted in the earth and our consciousness reaching for the highest heavens, we encompass the material and spiritual spheres, transforming matter into spirit and spirit into matter, as we ourselves are transformed. We become like a tree firmly rooted beside living waters, a tree whose fruit ripens and branches mature, giving life.

In the act of Lucid Surrender, with the assuredness of the Holy Tree, we discover unity in multiplicity, the universal within the personal, the magic and mystery nested in the holy branches of our dreams and within the reaches of our hearts.

NOTES:

7. Originally published as 'Lucid Surrender and the Holy Tree' in *Lucid Dreaming Experience*, 2, No. 3, December 2013, 8–9.
8. From W. B. Yeats' poem 'The Two Trees' in *William Butler Yeats: Selected Poems and Three Plays*, 4th edition, ed. M. L. Rosenthal (New York, NY: Scribner Paperback Poetry Edition, Simon & Schuster, Inc., 1996), 17–18.

Chapter 2

Lucid Dreaming and Lucid Surrender [9]

*Let the eye of your heart be opened
that you may see the spirit and behold invisible things.* [10]

— Ahmad Hatif (12th-century Sufi mystic)

Lucid dreaming, once dismissed by many in the scientific community, has now been mapped by Magnetic Resonance Imaging (MRI) and recognised as a specific brain state.[11] In 2009, neuroscientists first documented connections between reflective awareness in lucid dreams and the gamma brainwave frequency of 40Hz, associated with meditative states in contrast to the dreaming states of the sleep cycle.[12] Further, this higher range of 40Hz is most pronounced when the dreamer *does not attempt* to control the dream. Notably, when the lucid dreamer reports trying to control the dream narrative, the frequency has been shown to be slower, around 25Hz.[13] Lucid dreaming has been described as 'a trainable, meditative-like state developed while in sleep',[14] and in this book, I give a personal account of how this development can take place over time. The American Psychological Association (APA) has defined lucidity as occurring in 'a dream in which the sleeper is aware that he or she is dreaming and may be able to influence the progress of the dream narrative'.[15] Alongside this definition, there is an extensive literature on the secular phenomena of lucid dreaming, and how the dreamscape comprises a 'virtual reality' that allows the dreamer to create and enact scenes of their choosing, with the realism of waking life yet with none of the normal constraints. The dreamer can, for example, fly weightlessly, change physical form, and even have dream sex at will.[16] More recently, experiments have also demonstrated lucid dreaming's effectiveness in improving waking activities from music making to doing gymnastics,[17] while Hollywood films have brought lucid dreaming into popular culture.

Yet, the widely held view that the point of lucid dreaming is to be able to control the dream narrative limits the true potential of lucidity and does not account for the different levels of consciousness within the lucid state. We also need to explore and value the transformative effects that such experiences can have upon dreamers in their waking lives.

The practice of reflective awareness in dreams has a long history within spiritual traditions. Tibetan Buddhism, with its highly nuanced practice of Dream Yoga, is one such example.[18] The Abrahamic religions of Judaism, Christianity and Islam have all explored the revelatory aspects of reflective dreaming for spiritual purposes.[19] More recently, across the fields of Jungian and transpersonal psychology, the importance of yielding to a Greater Mystery is a shared touchstone.[20] Yet, in modern times, the connections between lucid dreaming, surrender and psycho-spiritual development have rarely been fully explored.[21]

In ordinary waking life, we perceive ourselves to exist in a single reality, bounded by space and time. However, in lucidity, we may find ourselves conscious of multiple dimensions of Being, as in the following dream — one I had some years into my practice of lucid dreaming, a time when I was also running a counselling centre:

I sit in a room where my dream teacher from waking life gives a lecture. Feeling very tired, I fall asleep as I listen, and in my dream-sleep, I become lucid. The dreamscape lifts like a veil and I find myself standing at the edge of a massive hall, the floor covered with a fiery-coloured Persian prayer rug. Surprisingly, numerous babies crawl around on the rug like little miracles of light. Even as I recognise the infants as representations of the Spirit's creative potential, they also remind me of my own longing to have a child.

On the opposite side of the hall spins a white light form set against glowing darkness. I am aware that, by means of Lucid Surrender, I can receive spiritual replenishment from this numinous Being of light.

As I stand observing the scene before me, I am aware of multiple dimensions at once: myself asleep on my bed; the lecture room in which the initial dream took place; the dream-sleep in which I became lucid; the hall full of babies; and the mystery of the spinning light form in the shining darkness.

Becoming aware of these five levels at once, I collapse to the floor and 'wake up', surprised to find myself back in the lecture room with others gathered around me. A dream Being, mimicking my hand movements, tells me, 'You were sitting there in a kind of trance speaking about how all five dimensions fit together.'[22]

Dream lucidity enacts the paradox of falling asleep to awaken, of 'losing' our life to find it. Becoming lucid while falling asleep within a dream, as happens in this example, signifies an actual shift in brainwave frequencies towards 'higher', more meditative states of consciousness.

Complex, multi-dimensional lucid dreams like this do not lend themselves to a simple operational definition focused on the dreamer's capacity to 'control' the dream. That is why I use the term *lucidity* to mean *a dream in which the dreamer becomes aware they dream, thereby releasing the transformative potential to experience new levels of awareness and depths of feeling compassionately enfolded within unifying consciousness*. Such an understanding of dream lucidity can encompass all the phenomena that may arise in dream lucidity, including Lucid Surrender.

The Practice of Lucid Surrender

In Lucid Surrender, I am conscious of the interleaving of worldly, exoteric knowledge with hidden, esoteric knowledge. Such discernment arises from alignment of my will with a Higher Will, rather than using this knowledge in the interests of my own will. In the course of hundreds of Lucid Surrender dreams, my readiness to relinquish my will has deepened over time, as reflected back to me by dream Beings like the one in this next example:

After a formless lucid dream in which I feel I've taken a bath in God, I find myself deposited in a normal dreamscape on a braided rug, at the feet of a matronly woman who sits in a rocking chair in front of a cosy fire. As I rest there, taking in what has happened, the woman leans over and asks me, 'What kind of lucid dreams are those when you let yourself be taken to God in this way?' I tell her, 'Surrender, the Path of Surrender.'

The 'path of surrender' raises the question: 'To what or to whom do we surrender?' Essentially one yields to the heartfelt recognition that 'I belong to more than myself.'[23]

Lucid Surrender reflects an inner attitude of heart and mind that not only acknowledges the transpersonal dimension but also expresses a longing akin to the song of the Psalmist: 'Like the deer that yearns for running springs, so my soul yearns for you, O God.'[24] I find the best way to prepare for dreaming is to quieten my mind and create a heart-centred focus that comes through meditation on the Lord's Prayer, a sacred song or a holy name. In my case, having been raised in the Christian faith, I call on the name of Elohim or Jesus, invoked in tandem with the rhythm of my breathing before falling asleep. Then, as lucidity dawns in the dream, the alignment of the heart with the Divine Will takes place through a simple act of surrender: waiting in meditative stillness with head bowed, knees bent in worship, and hands brought together in prayer, gestures that express the longing to know a deeper level of feeling and consciousness.

In lucidity, I have often felt surprised to hear myself spontaneously cry out, 'Take me to you, God!', expressed more poetically by the 11th-century Sufi mystic Ahmad Hatif, who writes: 'To Thee we surrender both heart and life and cast down both this and that before Thee. The heart is surrendered to Thee, since Thou art the ravisher of hearts...'[25] The response that follows depends not only on the emotional depth and simplicity of the desire held within the request but also on the dreamer's capacity to 'hold' what is revealed. As Hatif advises, 'Give all that you possess to Love. If your spirit is dissolved in the flames of Love, you will see that Love is the alchemy for spirit... you will journey beyond the narrow limitations of time and place and will pass into the infinite spaces of the Divine World...'[26]

Spiritual Encounters in Lucid Surrender

In lucidity, the dreamer who yields to the Transpersonal may find themselves face to face with numinous Beings of light, as I discovered in the following dream:

I look up and see a beautiful white ceiling with plaster-work butterflies and flowers. It occurs to me that this is a dream, and I become lucid. I wait quietly, and as I do so, the ceiling gives way to resplendent darkness on which I am carried a long way. I recall the Tibetan teaching that only the pure in heart can bypass the wrathful beings hidden in the darkness. Needful of protection, I sing a hymn to Jesus.

I become curious about what is carrying me so lovingly, and, as previously in lucidity, I yearn to 'see' this unseen presence. An invisible hand turns my head, and I realise that I am in the embrace of an angelic Being of golden, misty light.

> *This light holds me and infuses me with its qualities. I rest in wonder at the feeling of unutterable love that passes between us. It is as though we have become one, as I share in the Being's essence, its intelligence and regal nature.*
>
> *The mutuality of our awareness of each other as both one and separate suffuses our beings with joy and ecstatic pleasure. I am aware that I am being empowered for the service I have yet to complete in my life. Then I think, 'Where to?' But it has become hard to breathe. A voice says, 'Breathe through your mouth.' Doing so, I awake, breathing hard and deep.*

Encounters with such mysterious dream Beings are evocative of the profound Islamic teaching, 'I was a hidden treasure and I longed, I yearned, I loved to be known.'[27] The 'I' referred to here denotes not only one's own soul but also that of Absolute Being, which desires to be made known.

Such knowing may be conveyed through an unvoiced communication, as depicted in this dream:

> *After being carried on the Black Light by an unseen presence, I am set down in a still place on the radiant blackness. A man appears, wearing a sky-blue cloak and a white cape trimmed with orange over a white inner garment. A single large feather curves towards me above his head. He radiates a holy wisdom. I have the sense that he and I should embrace. I feel unworthy of this but obey.*
>
> *The moment my hands touch this man's shoulders and his mine, there erupts a great burst of energy that rushes into me and sends me catapulting back onto the rushing winds like a*

feather. I understand that a silent transmission or teaching has taken place and that the energy in this dream Being comes from the same Divine source as the light I have encountered in other lucid dreams.

In this instance, the dream Being's touch wordlessly transmits a 'spiritual science',[28] comprising Heart and Will — a 'more-than-human-consciousness'[29] — suffused with a light that illuminates my imagination and understanding. Such lucid dreams change our lives because they change our realisations, and our perceptions, about life.

In the chapters that follow, we will explore how the opening of 'the eye of the heart' in Lucid Surrender can expand our consciousness, illuminating our inner sight to reveal our spiritual potential and offering an infusion of wonderment and love that spills over into our waking world actions and relationships — a soul-awakening. In Lucid Surrender, the alignment of our consciousness with a Higher Will transforms the question 'Who am I?' into 'How can I best express this Will in the world with loving-kindness?' The sacred encounter does not end with the dream. Rather, it is fulfilled when the qualities of Soul are brought into waking life.

In lucidity, our ability to perceive the reality revealed to us through the 'eye of the heart' begins not in our personal mind, or ego, but in the depths of the soul. When, in the lucid state, we surrender with our minds and hearts, giving all that we possess to Love, we find ourselves taken on a journey beyond the narrow limitations of time and space to the unending reaches of Spirit.

Notes:

9. For a more extensive introduction to lucid dreaming and Lucid Surrender, see my previous book, *The Hidden Lives of Dreams*, particularly Chapter Ten (Bonnier Books, 2020).
10. Ahmad Hatif as referenced in *Essential Sufism*, eds. James Faiman and Robert Frager, foreword by Huston Smith (San Francisco, California: Harper Collings Publishers, 1997), 123.
11. Early research on lucid dreaming demonstrated that the dreamer can communicate with observers using agreed-upon eye movements during Rapid Eye Movement (REM) sleep. See Stephen La Berge, Lynn Nagel, William C. Dement and Vincent Zarcone, Jr., 'Lucid Dreaming Verified by Volitional Communication During REM Sleep', *Perceptual and Motor Skills*, 52 (1981): 727–732. However, research in 2009 by Allan Hobson and Ursula Voss measured the lucid state using MRI scans. See Ursula Voss et al., 'Lucid Dreaming: A State of Consciousness with Features of Both Waking and Non-Lucid Dreaming', *Sleep*, 32, No. 9 (1 September 2009): 1191-1200,https://www.ncbi.nlm.nih.gov/pmc/articles/PMC2737577/; and J. Allan Hobson, 'The Neurobiology of Consciousness: Lucid Dreaming Wakes Up,' *The International Journal of Dream Research*, 2, No. 2 (October 2009): 41–44.
12. See Ursula Voss and Allan Hobson, 'What is the State-of-the-Art on Lucid Dreaming? – Recent Advances and Further Questions' in *Open MIND*, eds. Thomas Metzinger and Jennifer M. Windt (Frankfurt am Main: MIND Group, 2015): 4, doi: 10.15502/9783958570306
13. Much remains to be learned about how the different frequencies are experienced in dreams and the types of cognition and emotion evident in each. Voss et al., 'What is the State-of-the-Art in Lucid Dreaming?', 14.
14. See James F. Pagel, 'The Synchronous Electrophysiology of Conscious States', *Dreaming*, 22, No. 3 (2012): 179, doi: 10.1037/a0029659
15. G. R. Vandenbos, ed. The APA Dictionary of Psychology (Washington, D.C.: American Psychological Association, Washington DC, 2007), 545.
16. For an introduction to the range of experiences within the lucid state, see Stephen LaBerge's Lucid Dreaming (New York, NY: Tarcher, 1985) and Robert Waggoner's Lucid Dreaming Gateway to the Inner Self (Moment Point Press: 2009).
17. See Melanie Schädlich and Daniel Erlacher, 'Lucid Music — A Pilot Study Exploring Experiences and Potentials of Music-Making in Lucid Dreams', *Dreaming*, 28, No. 3 (September 2018): 276–286, doi: 10.1037/drm 0000073. As an example of sports psychology in lucid dreaming, see the *Journal of Sports Sciences*, 'Effectiveness of Motor Practice in Lucid Dreams:

a Comparison with Physical and Mental Practice' (2015) by Tadas Stumbrys, Daniel Erlacher and Michael Schredl: http://www.tandfonline.com/doi/abs/10.1080/02640414.2015.1030342.
18. Choygal Namkhai Nrobu, *Dream Yoga and the Practice of Natural Light* (Ithaca, New York: Snow Lion Publications, 1992).
19. For a review of revelatory dreaming in Christianity, see Morton T. Kelsey's *God, Dreams, and Revelation: A Christian Interpretation of Dreams* (Augsburg Fortress: Augsburg Fortress Publishing, 1991, first published 1967). Henry Corbin provides an overview of theophanic dreaming in his *Swedenborg and Esoteric Islam: Comparative Spiritual Hermeneutics*, trans. Leonard Fox (West Chester, PA: Swedenborg Studies, 1995), and Kelly Bulkeley gives a wide-ranging overview in *Dreaming in the World's Religions: A Comparative History* (New York, NY: New York University Press, 2008). Catherine Shainberg's Kabbalah and the *Power of Dreaming: Awakening the Visionary Life* (Rochester, NY: Inner Traditions, 2005) provides a practical guide to the Kabbalistic tradition and revelatory dreams. For a thorough presentation of Jewish mysticism and practices, see *Kabbalah* by Gershom Scholem (New York, NY: Meridian, 1978).
20. For more on the relationship between Jungian Psychology and lucid dreaming, see 'Lucid Surrender and the Alchemical *Coniunctio*' by Mary Ziemer (Melinda Powell) in *Lucid Dreaming: New Perspectives on Consciousness in Sleep*, Vol. 2, eds. Kelly Bulkeley and Ryan Hurd (Santa Barbara, California: Praeger, 2014), 145–166.
21. For important examples of research into this type of lucid dreaming, see Fariba Bogzaran, 'Hyperspace Lucidity and Creative Consciousness' in Kelly Bulkeley and Ryan Hurd (eds), *Lucid Dreaming: New Perspectives on Consciousness in Sleep*, Vol. 2 (Santa Barbara, CA: Praeger, 2014), 209–231. See also Ted Esser's fascinating summary of his research on 'Kundalini and Non-Duality in the Lucid Dreaming State' in the same volume, 233–263. Ryan Hurd has explored 'Spontaneous Emergence: A Phenomenology of Lucid Dreaming' (Master's thesis, R. D. Hurd, 2008), http://www.driccpe.org.uk/?s=hurd. For seminal work on light in lucid dreaming, see Scott Sparrow, *Lucid Dreaming: Dawning of the Clear Light* (Virginia Beach, VA: Edgar Cayce Foundation, 1976) and George Gillespie, 'Light and Lucid Dreams: A Review', in *Dreaming*, 2, No. 3 (1992): 167–179, which provides an overview of his findings. Gillespie has also published a personal account of his lucid experiences, *Seeing: Beyond Dreaming to Religious Experiences of Light* (Exeter, UK: Imprint Academic, 2019). Further, for a dynamic, personal exploration of ecstatic lucid experiences, see Patricia Garfield, *Pathways to Ecstasy: The Way of the Dream Mandala* (New York, NY: Prentice Hall Press, 1979).

22. For more on dream-sleep states within lucidity see the chapter 'Shaman's Drum' in *Not for Innocent Ears: Traditions of a Desert Cahuilla Medicine Woman* by Ruby Modesto and Guy Mount, published in 1986 by Sweetlight Books, and Nrobu's *Dream Yoga and the Practice of Natural Light* (Ithaca, New York: Snow Lion Publications, 1992).
23. Powell, *The Ways of the Soul*, xvii.
24. From an adaptation of a sung version of Psalm 42:1.
25. James Fadiman and Robert Frager (eds.), *Essential Sufism*, 123.
26. Ibid.
27. From a *hadith* or teaching of the Prophet Mohammed cited in Henry Corbin, *Alone with the Alone: Creative Imagination in the Sufism of Ibn Arabi*, trans. Willard Trask (Princeton: Princeton University Press, 1969), 114.
28. Henry Corbin, *Swedenborg and Esoteric Islam: Comparative Spiritual Hermeneutics*, trans. Leonard Fox (West Chester, PA: Swedenborg Studies, 1999), 103. The term 'Spiritual Science' refers to a subtle knowledge of esoteric symbols and invisible reality.
29. The scientist Rupert Sheldrake uses this term in his book *Science and Spiritual Practices: Reconnecting Through Direct Experience* (London: Coronet, 2017), 21.

Chapter 3

ON LUCID SURRENDER: A PATH TO LUCIDITY [30]

I believe in the night.

— Rainer Maria Rilke [31]

Lucid dreaming as a concept came to my attention in 2006. Prior to that, I did not realise that the dreams I'd had since childhood skirted the edges of what I would now call lucidity. From the onset, lucidity involved a strange kind of Black Light that frightened me, apart from which, I did not trust the overpowering feelings that came with my dreams.

Even so, at the age of seven, in the 2nd grade, I do recall writing a story about a lucid dream in which, after many adventures, a prince and princess fly on a 'Lunderbird' to a magical castle in the clouds. The teacher had my mother come to school for a conference because she felt concerned about the 'precocious' nature of the story, wondering how I would ever think to write such a thing. After that, I kept the dreams to myself.

My mother, who raised me in the Baptist Church, sent me to a Christian kindergarten where children learned to read by memorising scripture — a process I relished. In school, I learned a host of sacred hymns and verses that I would repeat when afraid, sad or simply joyful. I loved psalms like 'The Lord is my Shepherd. I shall not want...' and felt the words as a continuation of beauty and light. This simple practice of repeating a sacred verse or song has carried over into my dreams.

I feel deeply grateful for such grounding in a sacred tradition. Unfortunately, though, the fearful anger of scripture affected me too. In my early teens (when I no longer feared the dark so much), I associated the strong winds, flight, levitation and whirring sounds that accompanied lucidity with demonic or evil powers — an idea rooted in the belief that it was permissible for biblical characters to have visions, but not a girl from Orange, California. This, together with the more dogmatic teachings of the church, caused me to close my heart to lucidity, and so I stopped the lucid dreams from happening until my late thirties. However, I still paid enough attention to my dreams in the meantime to follow their guidance.

My move from the United States to Europe in 1990 followed a semi-lucid dream in which, for the first time, I felt truly safe in the dark. This dream changed the trajectory of my life.

I still recall the exact circumstance of the day I had the dream. At that time, I had to make up my mind whether to accept an offer from the United States Peace Corps to go to Poland as part of the first group to enter the newly independent Eastern Europe or whether to stay in California and pursue my doctorate in English literature. At the university where I had taken my Master's degree in English literature and was working as a teaching associate, I had come across an advert from the United States Peace Corps for new recruits to help set up Teacher Training Colleges in Poland and Hungary. Soon thereafter, I applied and was invited to join the Peace Corps in Eastern Europe.

My mother, especially, had taken the news that I might go away quite hard. The day I told her of my plans she said, 'But if you go to Europe, you'll never come back!' I told her that she exaggerated, but thus far, her words have proven true, for, while I have since visited the United States many times, I have remained living in Europe.

On that day, my mother and I had a tearful conversation. To clear my mind and heart, I took a walk in the California foothills not far from home. Walking there, I found a bright yellow flower called a Brown-eyed Susan tucked within the brush. Pausing to eye the flower, I looked out over the ravine that I knew and loved well. Inwardly, I called out to the Lord to send me a dream to help me with the decision before me. Poland felt unexpected to me. Since I had minored in Spanish, taught in a bilingual school and studied Flamenco, I had imagined myself going to Spain or South America. Even so, having read a good deal of 20th-century Russian literature, especially from the Soviet era, I had followed the events leading up to the fall of the Berlin Wall in 1989 with great interest and felt very curious about life behind the former Iron Curtain.

The night of my walk in the foothills, I had the following dream:

> *At the base of the golden, California foothills, I wander through crowded carnival grounds, feeling alone. I only want a friend to go walking with me in the hills. The pressure of the crowds*

pushes me out into the hills where a man approaches me saying, 'I've heard that you've been looking for a friend.' His gentleness reassures me. I feel I can trust this stranger who wears a royal-blue poet's blouse and has wavy shoulder-length blond hair. His fine features and form radiate beauty.

As we walk in the hills, we communicate without words. The sea-washed breeze cools us. I ask him his name. He answers, 'Gabriel.' I turn to him and say, 'You know, that name means "Child of God".' He turns to me with a healing smile and says, 'I know.'

He invites me home to meet his family. His elderly parents and three sisters greet me warmly. A gentle fire burns in the hearth. They feed me freshly baked bread and fresh milk. I feel the meal makes me whole and gives me new life. After supper, Gabriel tells me that we will take a journey into the night. We get into his invisible 'car' and disappear at an incredible speed into a velvety blackness. With this I awake.

This dream foreshadowed my eventual experience of darkness in lucidity. Only later, in 2006, when I started my psychotherapy training at the Centre for Counselling and Psychotherapy Education (CCPE) in London, did I begin to understand the emotional issues and misconceptions that had kept me from trusting the lucid dreams.

The Inward Journey

Finding a psychotherapy training that suited me took a long time. After much soul-searching, I chose the transpersonal approach, one that takes spirituality — one's sense of values, purpose and meaning — into account, which was important to me. From this perspective, life crises and challenges become opportunities for creative change and growth. Dreams and the imagination serve as a way to understand our inner world, our essential nature and the world of Spirit.

At CCPE, we practised a dream re-entry technique developed by Nigel Hamilton, CCPE's Director, called the Waking Dream Process, in which we learned how to re-imagine our dreams with therapeutic guidance. The possibility of doing such work *within* an actual dream first dawned on me when I had the following dream:

> *I walk waist-deep in a creek at the base of the Eastern Sierras. Sunlight filters through the leafy covering, glimmering on the water's surface and the creek's golden sands. A few feet in front of me, a massive rainbow trout swims to the surface and remains still. I decide to catch the fish with my hands, the way my father and I used to do when I was young, but then I realise that the fish represents Spirit and stop myself. I noticed that the trout has turned on its side, revealing a rainbow. The fish looks exhausted. 'How' I ask myself, 'can the Spirit be weary?'*
>
> *It occurs to me that the fish also represents me. The thought comes to me that if I were awake and entering the dream through the waking dream process, then my dream guide would invite me to touch the fish. At that point, just as my finger comes to within a hair's breadth, the trout darts down into the water. Feeling disappointed, I awaken.*

Some months after the dream of the rainbow trout, I began

to become lucid more regularly and gained the confidence needed to 'let go' of the controls. A lucid dream from spring 2007 portrays this process:

> *Driving through the California foothills on a windy summer's day, I lose control of the car. It begins to veer off the side of the road at high speed. After a number of futile attempts to keep it on the road, I become aware I am dreaming and calmly make the decision to give up trying to control the car.*
>
> *The car goes faster and faster until it feels as if it has become a particle of light. At what seems the speed of light, the car hurtles towards a golden hillside, and everything blurs together. When the car slams into the hillside, my body and the dreamscape disappear. Everywhere becomes an expansive, shimmering blackness. An incredible pressure and noise centres between my 'brows', until all goes very silent and still. I know I have been dreaming, and I wonder if I have actually died during the dream. Although I am drawn to this infinite space, with this thought I wake up.*

In this early lucid dream, I didn't quite know what to make of it when my dream body and the dreamscape disappeared. Since that time, I have come to realise that in Lucid Surrender, a subtle body, one which may remain invisible or be revealed as light, with enhanced sensorial and intuitive capacities, replaces my usual dream body and mind. This I experience as the unveiling of 'Soul', the essence of my being.

Similarly, the light of the new dreamscape shines luminously like a black void, filled with living light. I describe this invisible light as 'living' because the light possesses a range of profound emotional tonalities. Out of this apparent void, the Black Light takes manifold forms: mineral, vegetable, animal, human, mental, angelic, Divine. Sometimes, when my soul gets taken into new dimensions of light, a new, visible dream body of light appears.

Three years later, in 2010, I had a more direct apprehension of this body of light, as in the following excerpt from a lucid dream:

> *After being carried a long way on the vibrant black winds, I see before me three very fine beams of golden laser light radiating from a vanishing point far off in the infinite blackness. The golden beams cross four fine arching beams of gold. At the points where the straight and curved beams meet, flashes of shimmering, diaphanous mist rise up. 'What is this?' I wonder. The answer that comes to me nearly takes my breath away: 'This is the structure of light, and I am travelling on light!' The beauty and truth of this vision fill me with humility. In this state, I feel I am being carried to the vanishing point. And then the thought comes: 'If I am travelling on light, then I must also be light!'*

I have a special interest in the appearance of light and colour in dreams in great part because I associate both with the presence of Spirit, as in this dream from 2008:

> *I stand at the checkout counter in a family market set in Lone Pine, California, at the base of Mt. Whitney. An elderly female cashier smiles at me as she tallies up the fresh bread and red*

wine I'd like to buy. When I notice the love in her eyes, I become aware the scene has become illuminated from within, bringing semi-lucidity. The woman turns left to look where a young man unpacks rainbow and golden trout for display. Watching the young man, I see a piercing white circle of light dance around him and the fish. The light follows my eye movement, not his, so I deduce it comes from me. With this, full lucidity comes, and I recognise the market as an image of my ego, mind or body, the light as Spirit. I feel jubilant as I bow my head and wait. The walls of the shop fall away and open into stars. I hear a familiar rush of powerful wind and feel my soul lifted onto the Black Light…

In waking life, I have long cultivated an attentive eye for what I think of as signs of the Spirit — hidden beauty, kindness, delightful incongruity and humour. My recognition of similar signs in my dreams often initiates lucidity.

Coming Home

When I pray before falling asleep, I sometimes enter lucidity through my prayers. By prayer, I mean a song of the heart akin to the idea of 'Centering Prayer' as taught by Father Keating[32] — taking a sacred hymn or name and repeating it in time with my breathing, syllable by syllable. Sufis say that when you find the breath, you find God. This feels true. The names and songs that I call on in prayer, and in my dreams, come from the Judeo-Christian tradition.

I am reminded of how St Teresa of Avila describes finding completeness with each breath when, in prayer, she repeats the name of the Lord. She discovers that this Holy name, her conception of God, takes her to a sacred, light-filled space. There she asks the Lord if his name serves as the only 'key' to this place. The answer comes:

> How old do you think is existence?
> For eons of time, souls have been entering Me;
> every Prophet's name is a key
> as is every heart full of
> forgiveness
> and love. [33]

The same is true in my own experience, as suggested by the following two dreams, the first from January 2009:

I wake up at 4 a.m. and pray. I start the repetition of the Holy Names with the breath. At some point, I feel a shift in my awareness, and I am dreaming. I find myself in the back garden of a friend from my teens. I walk towards the edge of the swimming pool and climb up on the back of a creature that I sense but do not see. As I sit there, a dark-haired man enters through the gate, backing a white horse into the space next to me. When the horse draws up next to me, I see it is a unicorn! With amazement, I think, 'But unicorns don't exist — or do they?' Leaning forward, I see a massive white horse's head with a single horn and realise I'm sitting on a unicorn!

With this, lucidity comes. I say, 'Okay, God. Here I am.' With a whoosh, my soul, alive with the ecstatic pleasure of the winds, is swept along a black tunnel. At last, I begin to see bright, pulsing lights ahead. They radiate out like enormous white orchid petals in a swirl of bloom. 'This time,' I think, 'I won't be afraid.'

Getting taken through the pulsing light takes a long time. Eventually, my being enters an immense, black-grey maelstrom that moves so fast, a tremendous pressure makes it hard to find my breath. The cloud has a beautiful texture with flecks of light in it. In response to the cloud's presence, I can only repeat 'Oh Holy One, Oh Holy One!' as I move into a black silent space, continually repeating, 'Oh Holy One, Oh Holy One.' I begin to wonder if I can ever get back, and in that instant, I am returned at speed, until I find myself back to the original dream, lying flat on my back on a green yoga mat next to the pool. The thought comes that I need to rest after what has happened, which I do in the dream, until I wake up.

A few years after this dream, I made a pilgrimage to Paris to see a series of legendary tapestries woven in the 1500s, known as *La Dame à la licorne* ('The Lady and the Unicorn'), housed in the medieval collection of the Musée de Cluny. Each of these six beautiful tapestries features a maiden, a unicorn and a lion, framed by an array of flora and fauna. They are displayed according to the traditional hierarchy of the senses followed in the Middle Ages, arranged left to right, moving from touch, taste, smell, hearing and sight to the sixth sense of the spiritual 'heart' — a movement inwards towards Soul. [34]

As I entered the darkened hall in which the softly lit tapestries are hung, a group of French school children gathered in front of the final and most enigmatic tapestry, called '*À Mon Seul Désir*', meaning 'My One Desire' or 'My

Will Alone'.[35] When the teacher referred to the unicorn, a boy raised his hand and said to his teacher in French, 'But unicorns don't exist!' His teacher leaned forward and said emphatically, 'That's right, unicorns don't exist, or do they?' and then proceeded with her description! Her comment, echoing my own thoughts in my unicorn dream, felt light-hearted and soulful.

In the second dream, which I had in 2011, my understanding of spiritual light deepens:

> *I am carried a long way down a tunnel illuminated with Black Light. Finally, the movement stops, and it feels as if my body rests on Holy ground in a foetal position on my right side. The black lies heavy over me like a thick blanket. My position has the feel of total and complete surrender. A part of me thinks, 'I guess life knows I need this.'*
>
> *A morning light surrounds me. It feels like pure light, somehow full of life's forms, and contains the sky, trees, birds, the earth and my being. The light has the musicality of water and air. I think for a brief moment that I've awakened to a sunny spring day and that I must be hearing sounds from outside. But then I understand the experience to be an actual awakening to what light truly is, and all that it contains. I feel like an apple on a grassy field, a creation of light, resting in the lucid space until the alarm wakes me up.*

This dream brings to mind the words of the poet Hafiz, when he has the sun confess:

> I am just a shadow.
> I wish I could show you
> The Infinite Incandescence (Tej)
> That has cast my brilliant image! [36]

Although I have learned to become more comfortable with Lucid Surrender, I still find such dreams challenging. The energy of the dreams can feel nuclear, and sometimes I get the feeling that the dreams have been 'training me up' for something yet to come.

I realise that not everyone will be attracted to the Divine as I portray in my dreams. To dreamers desirous of lucidity, I will say that I have found that calling the name of a person whose qualities are admirable also works, and that any song that puts the dreamer in touch with truly heartfelt feelings will create the right 'attunement' for Lucid Surrender. The revelatory power of Lucid Surrender can be overwhelming. Accordingly, I would recommend psycho-spiritual guidance as set out in the Appendix, and where possible, with the support of a dream guide.

The presence of angelic and Holy Beings in lucid dreams can also be understood as archetypes embodying truth, compassion, clarity, wisdom and beauty, attributes of the Divine, a topic I discuss further in Part II. These archetypal figures seem to exist independently, as well as in relation to each other, and, much to my surprise, in relation to me too, as illustrated in the following dream I had in 2012:

In the night, deep prayers move me. Spontaneously, I ask to be taken to the realm where spiritual Beings dwell in order to learn from them.

When I fall asleep, I dream the toilet at work has backed up again (as it has just done in waking life), and I realise this must be a dream! With lucidity, the ecstatic winds take hold of me. The journey continues with sharp, sudden changes that disorientate me, until a sung version of Psalm 38 springs to mind: 'You are my hiding place, you always fill my heart with songs of deliverance. Whenever I feel afraid, I will trust in you, I will trust in you, let the weak say I am strong in the strength of your love.' Finally, I pop into a space full of people wearing solid, coloured robes. They open a path between them leading to a quiet space where three men in coloured robes sit expectantly. I seem to know who they are. They exude a holy wisdom and appear to be awaiting me. Amidst their holiness, humanity, intelligence and love, I feel their interest and attentiveness. A sense of intimate, timeless communion arises between us. After some time, I am pulled back into waking consciousness.

Once awake, I cannot articulate what was communicated or exchanged; only the feeling quality lingers. I feel amazed to have had my request granted in this way.

I am very conscious that there is always more to learn in lucidity, and I am reminded of one lucid dream in which a Tibetan Buddhist, dream yoga teacher appeared. He explained that dreams unfold according to our capacity and what we bring to them. We can, he added, also build up our capacity for dreaming so that we may both give and receive.

Once this capacity is established, it continues to develop in response to the dreams as they bring greater depth of understanding to the dreamer. Most importantly, while the light of guidance may take embodied forms, the dreams themselves are the guides, serving like lanterns to light our path.

Notes:

30. This text is largely based on an interview hosted by the lucid dream teacher & author Robert Waggoner for his magazine *Lucid Dreaming Experience*, 1, No. 4 (March 2013): 2–12, as 'A Dreamspeak Interview with Robert Waggoner'.
31. Rainer Maria Rilke, *Rilke's Book of Hours: Love Poems from God*, I, 11, trans. Anita Barrows and Joanna Macy (New York: Riverhead Books, 1996), 57.
32. See http://www.centeringprayer.com for more on this form of prayer. I became familiar with teachings on Centering Prayer well into my experience of Lucid Surrender through the book *Centering Prayer and Inner Awakening* (Cambridge, Massachusetts: Cowley Publishing, 2004) by Cynthia Bourgeault. This form of prayer shares many resonances the simple prayerful meditation I do before sleep.
33. Quoted excerpts are from the poem 'Every Prophet's Name', trans. Daniel Ladinsky, *Love Poems from God: Twelve Sacred Voices from the East and West* (Penguin Group: New York, 2006), 272–273, used with permission. See Avila's *Interior Castle: The Classic Text with Spiritual Commentary*, C.Ss.R (Notre Dame, Indiana: Ave Marie Press, Inc., 2007). In this text, Avila describes how such states are accessed, their characteristics. However, in keeping with the medieval tradition of mystical theology in which she was steeped – and to deflect the suspicions of the Inquisition – she relates her visions through rhetorical devices such as extended analogies and metaphors rather than providing detailed descriptions. For an intriguing account of Avila's theology and style, see Peter Tyler's *Teresa of Avila: Doctor of the Soul* (London, UK: Bloomsbury Publishing, Plc., 2013).
34. This understanding of the series is laid out *The Lady and the Unicorn* by Elisabeth Delahaye, Director of the Musée de Cluny, when the book was originally published in 2007 (Paris: Editions de la Réunion de Musées Nationaux).
35. Ibid., 47.
36. Excerpt from 'My Brilliant Image', from *I Heard God Laughing: Poems of Hope and Joy: Renderings of Hafiz* by Daniel Ladinsky (London: Penguin Book Ltd., 2006), 7, used with permission.

Chapter 4

HEALING DREAMS IN LUCIDITY [37]

*But when I rest in emptiness,
my God is dark…*[38]

— Rainer Maria Rilke

In Old English the word for *healing* and *wholeness* share the same root. In this chapter, I would like to show how lucid dreams can be a powerful means of healing, providing the individual with the inward balance needed for physical and psycho-spiritual wholeness. For the healing process to be complete, the dreamer must then bring this inner wholeness into waking life.

This process can be usefully illustrated by the sand-painting rituals of the Navajo tradition in which a medicine man creates a sand painting in the form of a mandala, representing the internal balance that the ill person needs in order to achieve physical and psychological wholeness. The mandala is viewed as a living, spiritual entity, opening a connection to the spirit world. In the ceremony, the person seeking health sits at the centre of the mandala facing East, so that the spirits can bring medicinal agents while taking away the causes of illness and imbalance. Sands from the painting, or the 'visual prayer', are sprinkled on the patient as the medicine man sings holy chants.[39] In this way, the patient is brought into harmony with life. After the ceremony, the sand painting is destroyed so that no one can claim its ownership and power.

By analogy, lucid dreams, particularly those in which one surrenders, can be thought of as opening the dreamer to healing imagery, whose power none can claim.

As with the ceremonial mandala, restorative lucid dream imagery has an internal symmetry that serves to collect the dispersed elements of the psyche and establish internal balance in the dreamer. In the specific brain state of the lucid dream, a balance is struck between sleeping and waking mental processes.[40] As a result, the lucid dreamer, like a participant in the sand-painting ritual, can feel themselves between two worlds or indeed in a new one. I will illustrate how this can happen with three examples of lucid dream healing of body, mind and spirit based on my own experience.

This first lucid dream involves an actual physical cure. As a child and adult, I suffered from illnesses for which I have been fortunate to receive healing in dreams. One lucid dream stands out that not only restored my physical health but also changed the direction of my life. In June 2000, I moved from Switzerland to London, at a time of great personal sadness for me. I became severely ill with a sinus infection that infected my inner ear, debilitating me for weeks. Then I had the following lucid dream:

I stand in the afternoon light. A Being who reminds me of the angel Gabriel from a dream I had many years before approaches me and says, 'I hear you haven't been feeling well.' As he speaks, he lifts his right forefinger and touches my sinus areas under each eye. In the dream, I instantly feel better, and I realise that when I wake up, I will begin to get well. As he turns and walks away, I cry out to him, 'Can you heal my spirit?'

He turns and comes up to me again. He looks at me with a great deal of love as he raises his finger to the point between my eyebrows. His fingertip seems just a hair's breadth away from me, and I can feel its heat and power. Suddenly he looks at me very tenderly, and with great regret slowly lowers his hand as though he unexpectedly got a message not to heal me this way. We look long at each other, and I realise with disappointment and resignation that whereas the healing of my body would be rapid, the healing of my spirit would take years, at least seven years or more. And then I wake up.

As I sensed in the dream, I woke up feeling that I would recover. My physical recuperation was rapid. My spiritual renewal, as the dream foretold, took many years. However, the feeling tone of the dream gave me the resolve and fortitude I needed during a long, dry period in my life. The lucid dream also showed the steps that would be necessary to bring my inner being in line with my outer world. The illness and the dream articulated for me an inner need of which I had not previously been fully aware. Soon after the dream, I began to write a collection of stories from my childhood. Then I registered for studies in Psychology of Religion: the start of a lengthy training for psychotherapeutic work, and, thereby, the renewing of my spirit.

At the time, I had not learned that a lucid dream becomes profounder still if I 'surrender' by withdrawing my desire to directly control what happens as the dream unfolds. Nor did I realise that the opportunity for further healing would come through a series of lucid dreams. Subsequently, many dreams focused on the therapeutic resolution of mental complexes that had arisen from my conditioned responses to painful events that had taken place during my lifetime.

The lucid dream that follows came eight years after the previous one, not long after I'd taken on a new job as the Director of a charitable counselling centre. As Director, I was faced with the imminent closure of the centre due to an unexpected withdrawal of funding. The mental stress was very intense. The night of the dream was full of chaotic, dead-end thoughts as I tried to think my way through the crisis.

> *In the dream, I am on the busy, Southern California freeway system in a car driven by a woman I feel I know but can't recall. We are trying to get to a meeting about something important and meaningful to us. I realise that she is going about it the wrong way. She is lost in a tangle of overpasses and bypasses. I tell her she can take a more direct route if she gets off the freeway.*
>
> *Then the realisation comes in the dream that the freeways are like the mind's byways and that the situation is similar to how I feel in waking life. In that moment of lucidity, as I bow my head, the dreamscape falls away into blackness. My soul gets*

taken up by powerful winds at a slight upward angle until the space opens up, and I feel myself flat on my back, carried ever inwards down a shiny black tunnel.

As I am swept along, I think, 'Oh no, here I am out of my body again, and how will I get back?' There is an impatience about me, and I'm not really pleased to be in this situation. But just then, a voice says quite clearly, 'Come and be in my Being.' The words are comforting and inviting, and it seems clear I will get back, so I release my fear and yield to being carried in this way.

Eventually the space opens up, the winds cease, and my essence is placed inside a luminescent pearl with touches of mauve lining the light blue. I stay in this space for an eternal moment — enough to take in the spaciousness and silence, the sacredness and serenity, the still beauty of the life-giving light. I am surprised to be lifted out of this space — now that I am ready to stay! The return is like moving out from the centre point of a circle, out and out, and meeting my earthly body at the last moment.

This dream marked a shift in my understanding of the importance of surrender in lucid dreams, particularly the relinquishing of my fears and expectations. I woke up grateful for the experience yet shaking my head at the old habits of my mind and those ingrained pathways and fears that follow. This recognition was enough to begin to loosen my conditioned mind's hold over my thought processes.

Later, I recognised parallels to my own lucid dreams when I learned about the Clear Light or Clear Mind dreams described in the Tibetan Buddhist dream yoga tradition. In my dream, the Clear Mind state manifested as the pearl that 'the shell of time and space cannot contain'.[41] The lucid encounter with the lustrous, pearl-like light calmed my mind, giving me the sense of peace needed to meet the stresses of waking life with more equanimity and enabling me to handle the financial crisis facing the charity. Many times since, when I have been caught up in mental confusion, the lucid dream image of being within the inner pearl has served to centre and still my mind, so that my intuition can sense how best to heal the situation.

There have been times when a lucid dream has provided me with an immediate sense of spiritual rejuvenation, renewing my devotion to life. One such lucid dream came the night before I was given an injection to which I had a rare and severe allergic reaction:

As I walk down an empty London city street in the early morning, to my left I notice a wooden door slightly ajar, and I enter. It opens into a small, softly lit shop. A handsome man, slightly older than me, is dozing behind the counter and wakes up as I enter. It surprises me to see that a bed takes up most of the shop. A thick, rumpled, golden cover drapes over the bed, and its velvet folds catch the light and shadows in a mesmerising way. The man is a jeweller, and he tells me he's made a 'bauble' for my mother. He says this as though she is alive, though she had actually died a few years before.

As he holds the bauble up to the light, I see it is made of large solid gold squares hung around a gold chain. He asks, 'Isn't her name Margid or Majid?' 'Margaret,' I reply. 'Oh yes, that's it,' he responds. Aware that I don't have enough money to buy this priceless necklace, I ask if my mother has paid the deposit. 'She has already paid the full price,' he tells me, and smiles. He moves to the bed, where I notice a clock that reads 6.30 a.m.

I realise that it is really 6.30 in the morning and become lucid. Jubilant, I bow my head and wait breathlessly. In an instant, the dreamscape falls away and it feels as if my soul rises above my physical body and into my chest with a roaring sound. I am carried backwards on a current of wind across the Black Light, this time at an incredible speed, faster and further than ever before, between flashes of light and darkness. There is a moment of panic until I hear the holy name of Gabriel and begin to repeat it.

With this, I become calm, and two invisible presences take me through a countless expanse of stars. The stars are intelligent, radiant and full of life, like breath-takingly beautiful Beings of light. They seem countless and endless, yet each one is unique. Then I see that the stars encircle an immense, numinous black centre that they worship and reflect as they orbit slowly around. The two unseen presences lead me into the very centre of this vast, shining blackness. There they leave me hovering in a still space that is firm and supple at the same time.

For a moment I feel bereft, lost, as if there is no way to know what this mystery is or who I am. But recalling the velvety darkness of other dreams, I wait for a long time, repeating the sacred name until it becomes clear to me that this shining blackness is actually supporting and sustaining me — giving me life. So how could it harm me? I feel one with the *mysterious, soft, sacred darkness and at the same time found, known and loved. As the Black Light moves through me I feel that I, too, can know and love.*

I am moved to dance. Raising my right arm up into Natarajasana — the Lord Shiva's Dance pose in yoga — I notice that my arm is a beam of light. I am the fullness of joy, alive with the inner light of this black Holy mystery and the multitude of worshipping stars.

At this moment, the two presences lift me up and guide me back through the stars to my earthly body in London, where I live in daily life. I feel rested and safe, sure that all will be well. I awaken and it is 7 in the morning.

In such lucid dreams, I have developed an appreciation of the healing power held in what I describe as 'Black Light'. I have learned to trust that this light acts as a guide. The 15th-century mystic and priest St John of the Cross wrote, 'Oh Night, my guide! Oh Night, more loving than the dawn.'[43] Could it be that St John too is speaking of an encounter with the Black Light?

The Black Light teaches me how to be in the lucid dream space. Sometimes a voice speaks out of the shining darkness reminding me to breathe or to simply be. Many times, the Black Light has revealed itself in a revelatory vision of form, colour and light, as in the lucid dream of the pearl. At other times, it simply holds me and infuses me with qualities that I may need, like strength, courage, patience or compassion. In Lucid Surrender, when the Black Light appears, it feels like my soul and the Black Light become one.

Such lucid dreams of wholeness, of returning to the 'Source

of Light',[44] do not mean that life is intended to be one of ease. On the contrary, it feels that such dreams often come prior to a period that proves to be extremely challenging. Yet lucid dreams can imbue the dreamer with the grace to meet and contain difficult waking-life situations.

Like the centre point that unifies the mandala, a lucid dream can take us to the mysterious centre that is the source of our being and our wholeness. Like the practice of the Navajo sand-painting ritual, Lucid Surrender transports us to our innermost being, the place where we can find healing for body, mind and soul.

NOTES:

37. Originally published as 'The Healing Sands of Lucid Dreamtime' in the *Lucid Dream Exchange*, No. 58 (March 2011): 12–16.
38. This is my own translation from the German. See the original version in *Das Stunden Buch* by Rainer Maria Rilke (Berlin, Germany: Insel Verlag, 1996), 11–12.
39. David Villaseñor, *Tapestries in Sand: The Spirit of Indian Sand Painting* (Happy Camp, California: Natluregraph Company Publishers, Inc., 1966), 7.
40. J. Allan Hobson, 'The Neurobiology of Consciousness: Lucid Dreaming Wakes Up', *The International Journal of Dream Research*, 2, No. 2 (October 2009): 41–44.
41. A line from the poet Hafiz, quoted in *The Penguin Dictionary of Symbols*, Jean Chevalier and Alain Gheerbrant, trans. John Buchanan-Brown (London: Penguin Books, 1996), 745.
42. Before this particular lucid dream, I had done a Sufi meditation on the quality of *majid*, Arabic for 'majesty' while on retreat.
43. For the original Spanish text, see *St John of the Cross (San Juan de la Cruz): Alchemist of the Soul: His Life, His Poetry, His Prose*, trans. and with commentary by Antonio T. de Nicolás (York Beach, Maine: Samuel Weisser, Inc., 1989).
44. From Lao Tzu's Tao Te Ching, beautifully translated by Stephen Mitchell (New York, NY: Harper Perennial Modern Classics, 2006), no. 52.

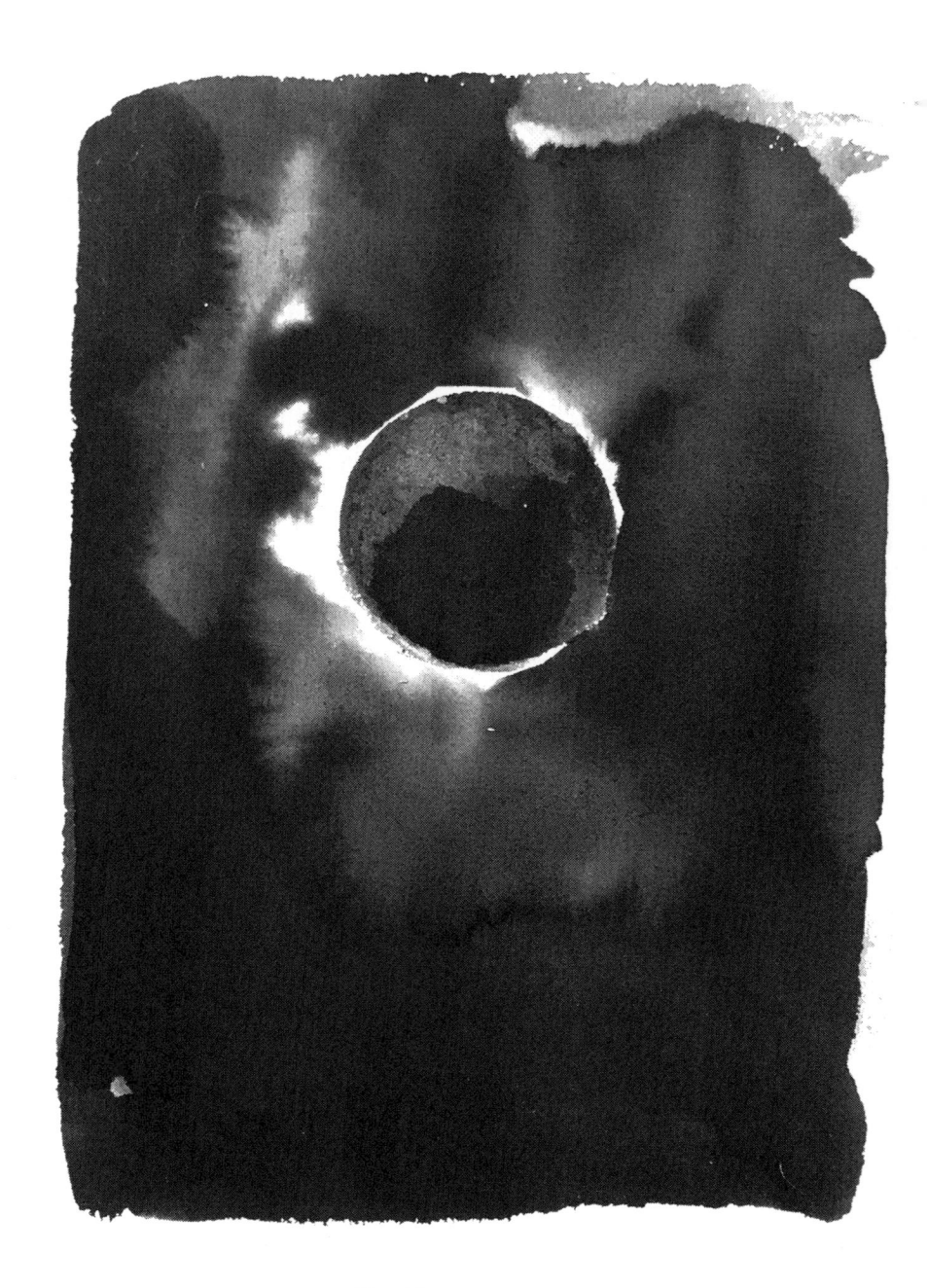

THE BLACK SUN

Part II

Awake in Sleep!
Lucid Dream Alchemy

*If your spirit is dissolved in the flames of Love,
you will see that Love is the alchemy for Spirit.* [45]

— Ahmad Hatif (11th-century Sufi mystic)

Chapter 5

THE ALCHEMIST'S STUDY: LUCID DREAM ALCHEMY [46]

He who denies true dreams, speaks in a dream. [47]

— Heinrich Khunrath

Lucid Dream Alchemy explores lucid dreaming through the twin lenses of alchemy and Lucid Surrender. A debt is owed to Carl Jung, the founder of analytical psychology, who understood alchemical imagery to be revealing of the process of Individuation, whereby a person's outer life becomes creatively aligned with their inner nature.

The alchemy of transpersonal consciousness, in which the practice of Lucid Surrender confers a profound experience of wholeness within the dream, can be signposted by key stages and symbols outlined in Jung's alchemical model. This chapter introduces alchemical emblems and principles that help us to understand the transformational processes at work in dream lucidity. Further chapters in this section amplify the alchemical teachings introduced here as they express lucid dream alchemy.

Figure 1. The Alchemist's Study (1595)

Awake in Sleep: The Alchemist's Study

While learning about alchemy and becoming familiar with lucid dreaming during my psychotherapy training, I came across a 16th-century alchemical emblem by Heinrich Khunrath entitled *The Amphitheatre of Eternal Wisdom* (*Amphitheatrum Sapientiae Aeternae*), popularly known as 'The Alchemist's Study' (Figure 1). When studying this work, I realised that this and other alchemical illustrations use imagery to encode a narrative for the spiritual process at work in Lucid Surrender — no less than a lucid dream alchemy.

I invite you now to reflect on Khunrath's engraving in which we find keys to understanding the inner state required to initiate and sustain Lucid Surrender.[48]

At the centre of this emblem, over the arching doorway, are inscribed the words, *Dormiens Vigila*, 'Awake in Sleep' (Figure 2). These words can be taken as a call to 'wake up' and to live more attentively in daily life. Equally, this injunction can be understood as an invitation to become lucid while dreaming.

Figure 2. *Dormiens Vigila*

Both kinds of wakefulness open us to an attentiveness to the mystery of life. As Khunrath observed, through 'hypnotic Visions or dream-Revelations, the soul can undertake to understand and explain the secrets of the whole created Universe..., to be united with good Spirits; to recount things past, contemplate Present Events, [and] presage those to come.'[49]

Across cultures, alchemical emblems provide templates for understanding and accessing archetypes of transcendence. For example, in ancient Chinese alchemy the image of the Tao — the Undivided One — stands supreme. From this Tao arises form, represented by the duality of *Yin* and *Yang* (Figure 3).

Figure 3. *Tai Ji* (*Yin* and *Yang*)

Similarly, there are two complementary aspects to the Khunrath emblem. On the left, there is the curtained oratory or chapel, where the alchemist kneels in reverential surrender to God; on the right, the alchemist's laboratory, in which the alchemist devotes himself to the creation of the *Lapis Philosophorum* or Philosopher's Stone, an enigmatic substance purported to transform the denseness of lead into pure gold. Yet the medieval alchemists understood that the Stone could do much more than this — that it comprised a *medicinam propium* — a special or proper medicine. This medicine, also called the elixir of life, was said to heal all manner of wounds, both outer and inner. [50]

Notice that the word *laboratory* is formed from the Latin roots of *labour* (work) and *orare* (pray). The alchemist's great endeavour is founded on reason and experience, words carved on the two pillars at the foreground of the laboratory, where the alchemist's chemicals are stored. [51]

A table in the middle of the study is covered with sheets of music and musical instruments, intimating the principles of symmetrical proportion and harmony. The plaque at the front of the table reads, 'Music dispels melancholy and banishes demons.' (I have found this to be true in my lucid dreams, in which sacred songs calm me, sustain lucidity and provide protection.) The music-strewn table demarcates the line between the laboratory and oratory — between rational and intuitive ways of knowing. In lucidity, the dual attributes of 'laboratory' and 'oratory' prepare the lucid dreamer for the reality of Lucid Surrender. The merging of the objective and subjective opens up the dreamer to a new threshold of consciousness — potentially transformative lucidity.

In Lucid Surrender the dreamer must still the mind and voluntarily relinquish their will to the Higher, Divine Will. I see Khunrath's study as emblematic of entering this 'higher', more focused state — opening a door to a new dimension. A quote from Ibn al-'Arabi, the 12th-century Persian philosopher and mystic, conveys this decisive moment poetically: 'My heart clings to the door of the Divine Presence, waiting mindfully for what comes when the door is opened.' [52] Similarly, Jung observed that 'The dream is a little hidden door in the innermost and most secret recesses of the soul, opening into that cosmic night...' [53] As the emblem suggests, when crossing this threshold in Lucid Surrender, an attitude of humility and wonder is required. Two key questions arise: What does surrender in lucid dreams entail? And to what does the lucid dreamer surrender? Alchemical emblems guide us as we seek answers to these questions.

The Path of Surrender

In Lucid Surrender, the aim is to relinquish the personal, finite ego in favour of what Jung called the larger self or the transpersonal aspect of Being. This calls for both humbleness and confidence, a recognition of one's personal limitations, yet daring to enter the vast mystery of the universe, without and within.

When I become lucid, sometimes, like the alchemist in his oratory, I fall to my knees. Other times, I simply bow my head in prayer or say, 'Here I am, if you want me, Lord.' Upon which, the original dreamscape disappears, giving way to an expanse of luminescent Black Light. My soul is seized by the shining darkness and the winds that accompany it. From this point on, rather than trying to control what happens, my role is simply to surrender my will by quieting my mind and being humbly present to what arises. To help overcome my fears and maintain a sacred focus, I repeat a holy name or sing a sacred song from the spiritual faith in which I was brought up, namely, Christianity.

The following dream illustrates this process:

I walk along the sea, passing by a large granite stone with a streak of vibrant green moss running along the centre from top to bottom. I stop to admire the green. When I touch the moss, an intense joy runs through me as I realise that the green is the Holy Spirit.

Perceiving this, I become lucid. The dreamscape and my dream body disappear. Carried on illumined black winds, I sing a holy hymn. When the speed slows, I find myself in a space filled with geometric light forms. I say to myself, 'Now I am in Plato's realm of ideal forms.'

Then I am carried through an immense tunnel consisting of light. At the far end, tubular light forms, resembling crystal organ pipes, emit a white light. The rays rain down on me like music, and when they touch the crown of my head, all sense of separation disappears. The light fills me, purifies, cleanses and renews me. But more than just my being is filled. Life itself is replenished.

My consciousness shifts, and I re-enter the original dream, back on the beach where I had been walking. I awaken from the dream.

This dream bears several hallmarks of Lucid Surrender. In the dream, my attentiveness to the colour green, combined with my longing to be filled with Spirit, spark lucidity. I sustain a devotional quality by singing a sacred song to still my mind, as the winds carry me into the mysterious darkness. Doing so requires that I keep focused, rather than becoming distracted, as the riches of the inner world are revealed. This concentrated focus sustains lucidity. As my concentration intensifies, so does my lucid state, in which I am carried through a tunnel into a new dimension. Here, my task is to receive the light, to be receptive to the transforming love that is the alchemy of the Spirit. I arise from sleep, ready to bring this love into the day ahead.

The medieval mystic St. Teresa of Avila has written of the Divine Presence in visions, and her words resonate with my realisation of Lucid Surrender:

> One Divine Being is existence.
> All the forests on this earth combined are but
> A tiny wood fiber – a particle of one spoke
> on the Wheel.
> What is the relationship of form
> to the unseen aspects of God?
>
> What percentage of God is unseen?
> What percentage of the Truth of Him do we know?
>
> He led me to a place where only Light existed... [54]

The Sufi teacher Pir Vilayat Inayat Khan reminds us that although Avila's revelations were unbounded by time and space, she engaged in a down-to-earth way with the needs of the mundane world. Khan's criterion for the mystic applies equally to the lucid dreamer: 'to be able to cross the threshold and still find one's way back into the world of time and space, to bridge the two…through creativity and service to life.' [55]

Lucid Dreams and Alchemical Emblems

A few essential alchemical emblems help to illuminate the spiritual transformation that unfolds on the path of Lucid Surrender. I begin with the ouroboros, the alchemical snake, which, as a symbol of life's constant regeneration, eternally eats its own tail. The circular form of the ouroboros, as shown here in a 1st-century alchemical drawing, [56] not only depicts life's eternal cycle of birth, death and resurrection, but also the reconciliation of opposites. The Greek text in the centre reads 'the all is one'. In ancient Egypt the ouroboros represented the belief that the sun's solar disc was re-filled every night, a powerful symbol for the spiritual replenishment that takes place each night as we dream.

Figure 4. The Ouroboros

The Four-Fold Spheres, from Michael Maier's *Atalanta Fugiens* (1618),[57] represents the completion of the Great Work of alchemy — the transformation of the base material of our lives into pure wisdom (Figure 5). This is illustrated by four spheres — the number four being the symbol of completion.

Figure 5. The Four-Fold Spheres

The spheres traditionally appear in the sequence of the four key alchemical colours, from bottom to top: black, white, yellow and red. Each can be understood as depicting a stage in a person's psycho-spiritual development. The magnificent spheres hover over the water, illumined by an eternal flame, as if to suggest subtle dimensions of awareness.

In the alchemical model, the first circle, coloured black,

represents the dense blackness of *Nigredo*, from the Latin, or *the blackening* that characterises the base matter of our lives (the unconscious conditioning and complexes that shape our view of reality). Not only does all this need to be made conscious in order to be integrated and mastered, memories must also be re-imagined, viewed with compassion for ourselves and others. As we work creatively through our negative patterns, the darkness reveals a luminescence, a growing spiritual perception that, as described in the dream that opens this chapter, inspires joy rather than despair.

Going through life, inevitably painful at times, we become aware of what matters most to us, not just on the surface but at a deeper level of value and purpose — the level of soul. The broadening of this self-understanding takes place in the next stage of the alchemical process, known as *the Albedo* or *the whitening*, in which we come to a more compassionate understanding of our soul nature. (In alchemy, this soulful awareness is associated with the moon's whiteness.) As our dreams become clearer and more lucid, like the waxing moon, the simplicity and intensity of Albedo imagery intensifies, as happened in a dream I had when I was ill one Christmas holiday:

In the dream, I am at work, but realise that I am actually still on holiday. I say to the Lord, 'Here I am if you want to take me.' With lucidity, the dreamscape falls away and opens to the Black Light and a strong currant of wind. It is hard to keep my focus on a sacred song. My soul is taken into an immense lavender cloud of light. The cloud has a fulsome gentle quality of indescribable beauty — very fine, delicate, subtle yet strong. I descend through this lavender cloud. When the downward movement ceases, I see below me white panels with beautiful patterns carved into them, and am aware that it's best not to try too hard to study them but rather to intuit their meaning.

I remain suspended in a stream of violet light while 'reading' the white squares, which feels calming and cleasing.

In the alchemical sequence, *Albedo* leads to the stage of *the yellowing*, in which we surrender our nature to a larger life purpose, greater than the individual ego can comprehend. In *Citrinitas*, we develop the spiritual qualities we need as individuals to become servants of life itself. Here we learn to transform our instincts and fears — the sulphurous material to which alchemists referred — into the gold of a truly mature personality.

At this stage of Lucid Surrender, there comes an intimate sense of union with the Divine. Much as the moon reflects the light of the sun, the living forms of light mirror not only the dreamer's inner state but also that of Spirit. In the dream that follows, at a time when I was feeling dispirited by a challenging time at work, I encounter such a light form:

I walk with a co-worker in a beautiful Gothic town. A fine misty rain falls, and so I invite her to the counselling centre that I direct. When we enter the centre, it looks completely different, composed of a large banqueting hall that contains a U-shaped table.

Employees and clients from the counselling centre are

seated along the long sides of the table while I sit on my own in the middle section. I rest my head on the white tablecloth and, as weariness overwhelms me, give in to the desire to sleep. Realising that I have fallen into a deep sleep within a dream, I become lucid.

I find myself lovingly carried into a soft, sublime darkness, where I remain for some time, while an ecstatic vibration runs through me. Abruptly, at great speed, I am taken across a threshold into the middle of an interlaced web of repeating series of numbers from 1 to 10, extending out in endless white spirals all around me, like the central florets of a sunflower, set against a brilliant black backdrop.

The white numbers feel alive. They pulsate and dance, carried joyfully on the same wind that supports me. Some numbers appear to rise up in response to an unheard rhythm, in alternating sequences of odd and even numbers. It occurs to me that I am being shown a mysterious code that lies behind the universe. Now, the numbers begin to turn into dancing black notes. After an eternal moment, the entire scene gives way to a bright blackness that resonates with the sound of a woman's voice as she sings a beautiful song to the accompaniment of a lute.

The sound moves through me like pure water, bringing the awareness that this music supports and gives life to all I have seen, in the dream and in waking world. The woman sings, 'Lay down your soul when you are tired, and rest your heart in God's desire.' Filled with such yearning, I am abruptly carried back through the blackness and re-enter my sleeping dream body. I 'wake up' still lucid within the initial dream, seated at the table, *feeling relieved and grateful that the others have left me to my dream within a dream undisturbed. A colleague offers me a warm Christmas drink.*

Intrigued by the spiralling pattern of number sequences, I later learned that the pattern of the seed-bearing florets of the sunflower express a mathematical formula called the Fibonacci sequence. The angle of this spiral conforms to the 'Golden Ratio', found at the heart of many natural forms. In the sunflower, this ratio optimises the number of seeds the flower can contain. By maintaining a devotional focus in Lucid Surrender, my own capacity to contain the awe-inspiring and deeply moving experience is enhanced, and like the sunflower that turns towards the sun, my heart turns towards Spirit. In lucidity, *Citrinitas* light forms encountered in lucidity expand our capacity to hold powerful feelings and widen our perspective on life, giving us soul stamina.

Dreams such as this one remind me of a teaching given by Abd al-Qadir in the 12th century. He describes the human heart as possessing two eyes: one that sees the realm of forms in manifestation revealed by the outer light; and one that sees 'only that which is rendered by the light of unity and oneness'.[58] In *Citrinitas*, it feels like the lucid dreamer can hope to see simultaneously with both eyes of the heart.

The final stage of the alchemical process, denoted by the uppermost red sphere, indicates a profound and loving re-engagement with life itself. In this stage, known as *Rubedo* or *the reddening*, a new, multi-faceted understanding of ourselves and the world enters into our earthly life, the fruit of all we have learned in the Alchemist's Study.

In line with the teachings of ancient alchemy, the dreamer must forego the personal ambitions of the ego in order to yield to the Divine, 'The Great Alchemist'. The path is one of praise, supplication, thanksgiving, a dedication to daily work and humble devotion, guided by the twin pillars of reason and experience. As with the Great Work of Alchemy, so it is with the practice of Lucid Surrender: a sacred art in the service of soul.

NOTES:

45. Hatif, *Essential Sufism*, 123.2.
46. This text first appeared in my 2008 Lucid Dream Alchemy website, which is no longer online.
47. Quoted in Peter J. Forshaw, '"Behold, the dreamer cometh": Hyperphysical Magic and Deific Visions in an Early-Modern Theosophical Lab-Oratory', in *Conversations with Angels: Essays Towards a History of Spiritual Communication, 1100–1700*, ed. Joad Raymond, 175–200 (UK: Palgrave, Macmillan, 2011), used by Khunrath in the 1609 edition of *The Amphitheatre of Eternal Wisdom*, is attributed to Julius Caesar Scalinger. See endnote no. 1, 189.
48. Engraving by Hans Vredeman de Vries, Public domain, via Wikimedia Commons.
49. Forshaw, 'Behold, the dreamer cometh', 187.
50. For more on how the Philosopher's Stone may relate to lucid dreaming, see Ed Kellogg's and Mary Ziemer's [Melinda Powell], 'Lucid Dream Alchemy: The Making of the Philosopher's Stone', presented at the International Association for the Study of Dreams Psiber Dreaming Conference, 2014, https://www.academia.edu/18468306/Lucid_Dream_Alchemy_Making_the_Philosophers_Stone.
51. Andrea De Pascalis, *Alchemy the Golden Art: The Secrets of the Oldest Enigma* (Gremese International: Rome, 1995), 104–105.
52. As cited by Stephen Hirtenstein in his article 'Muhyiddin Ibn 'Arabi: The Treasure of Compassion', passage 1.59 from the *Futuhat*, trans. William Chittick in *Beshara*, No. 12 (Autumn/Winter 1990): 30–38, http://besharamagazine.org/wp-content/uploads/2016/10/Issue-12-clear.pdf

53. E. C. Whitmont and S. Brinton Perera, *Dreams: A Portal to the Source* (London: Brunner-Routledge, 1989, 1994), 18.
54. Ladinsky, *Love Poems from God*, 'Every Prophet's Name', 272–273, used with permission
55. Pir Vilayat Inayat Khan, *Introducing Spirituality into Counselling & Therapy* Omega Publications: New Lebanon, New York, 1969, 1982), 162.
56. This drawing is attributed to Cleopatra the Alchemist in the text the *Chrisopoeia of Cleopatra* or the *Gold-making of Cleopatra*.
57. Michael Maier's *Atalanta Fugiens: Sources of an Alchemical Book of Emblems*, originally published in 1617, ed. H. M. E. De Jong (York Beach, ME: Nicolas-Hays Inc., 2002), Figure 17, entitled 'A four-fold fireball controls the work', 393, Michael Maier, Public domain, via Wikimedia Commons.
58. Hadrat Abd al-Qadir al-Jilani, *The Secret of Secrets*, trans. Shaykh Tosun Bayrak al-Jerrahi al-Halveti (The Islamic Text Society: Cambridge, 1991), 56.

Chapter 6

The Fullness of the Void: Black Light in Lucid Surrender [59]

Oh happy gate of blackness,
which art the passage to this so glorious change! [60]

— Sir George Ripley (15th-century alchemist)

What is Black Light? Imagine taking part in a physics experiment in which you are asked to peer into a box full of natural light. What would you see? The light contained in the box would appear as black emptiness because, to human eyes, light is invisible. However, if a metal wand were inserted into one side of the box and spun around, flashes of metal would become visible, while the light, however, remains unseen.

We see only the objects light illuminates. [61] This is why, once beyond the earth's atmosphere, the apparently empty reaches of outer space appear black. To be perceived visually, light wavelengths must inter-penetrate with matter. Physicists believe that matter, from the smallest grain of sand to the largest galaxy, forms only five percent of the universe, with invisible dark matter and dark energy comprising the remaining ninety-five percent. [62]

Prefiguring this discovery, the ancient alchemical precept 'As above, so below' [63] describes ordinary waking consciousness as representing only a minute fraction of an infinitely larger, 'spiritual' universe, from which material reality arises. In the words of the medieval alchemist Michael Sendivogius, we learn to see that 'this natural world is only an image and material copy of a heavenly and spiritual pattern; that the very existence of this world is based upon the reality of the celestial archetype; and that God had created it in imitation of the spiritual and invisible universe.' [64] The invisible realm is thus seen in 'Nature as reflected in a mirror'. [65]

In the alchemical worldview, just as there is a physical sun, so there is a spiritual sun, illuminating the mind with understanding. Alchemists depicted this sun as the *sol niger*, the black sun, suggestive of inner mysteries, in contrast to the sun by day, associated with rational thought. [66]

In the natural world, a full solar eclipse creates a seemingly 'black sun' that radiates a halo of light, a striking display of darkness and light, a juxtaposition of opposites. Alchemically speaking, the alignment of the earth, sun and moon mirrors a profound alignment of body, soul and spirit.

Before I knew about the alchemical teachings on the *sol niger*, I had the following Lucid Surrender dream, portraying an encounter with the black sun:

With lucidity, I bow my head and the dreamscape and my dream body give way to Black Light. Strong winds on the blackness

> *carry me as if I were lying on a flying carpet moving at the speed of light. Staying with this movement takes a good deal of energy. To help keep my focus I repeat a sacred song. Far in the distance, I am astounded to see what looks like a black sun. The sun becomes ever larger upon approach. Eventually, the movement slows, and I find myself set down before this immense, living sun.*
>
> *The sun's wavy rays are outlined in a thin band of reddish-orange. As the rays break off, moving into the blackness in wavy lines, new ones appear. The beauty and power fills me with wonder. I perceive the sun's profound presence to be Divine and ask, 'Why a black sun? Why this way?' The answer: 'So you won't be annihilated.'*
>
> *Without warning, a ray strikes me in my heart area, filling me with bliss. I cry out with joy, aware of this light's beauty and truth. The ray's power moves through me making me cry out with longing, 'Give me the ability to love and heal!' When I connect with this desire the sun dissolves into deep red, as I awaken.*

In this dream, it felt as if my ego, along with all its drives and defences, had been eclipsed so that I could be opened to a greater reality, (although I yet desired a spiritual gift!).

Later, I learned that Sufi mystics describe a place called 'The Land of the Midnight Sun', where Black Light shines. Of such light, the narrator of the 14th-century Persian medieval poem, *The Rose Garden of Mystery*, movingly speaks:

> Blackness, if you but knew, is the Light of Essence;
> Within the essence flows the Water of Life …
>
> What can I say about this most subtle secret
> of a luminous night within a dark day?[67]

This light, perceived by the organ of inner sight, the heart,[68] heralds a revelation of the Divine or 'supra-consciousness'.[69]

Black Light illuminates the teachings of many mystical traditions across the world. To understand its nature as revealed in lucidity, and the spiritual importance it holds for humanity today, I will draw on the concept of alchemy described by Carl Jung and on the teachings of the wisdom traditions.

The Alchemical Model in Psychotherapy

Jung drew parallels between the development of the human psyche, as it came to be understood in the early 20th century, and alchemy. He recognised that the alchemical pursuit to transform base matter into gold combined both physical and spiritual alchemy, the alchemists themselves undergoing psycho-spiritual transformation while conducting their experiments.

Jung de-codified many richly illustrated alchemical emblems to show not only how they portray the secrets of physical alchemy but also psychological stages of maturation, evident in waking consciousness *and* dreams. The alchemical process manifests on two levels, known as the Lesser and the Greater Wisdom. The first refers to knowledge of the earthly world, the second to knowledge of the spiritual. Jung brought the two forms of knowing together in his alchemical studies on the psychological and spiritual development of Individuation, a process by means of which a person matures in body, psyche (or soul) and spirit. In formulating this concept, Jung drew on the alchemical stages outlined in Chapter Five: *Nigredo, Albedo, Citrinitas* and *Rubedo* (*the darkening, the whitening, the yellowing* and *the reddening*). In exploring Black Light, we will be focusing on the first of these: *Nigredo*.

In Jung's alchemical model, working through 'dark' or challenging times, when external forces beyond our control shatter our sense of who we are, compels us to acknowledge our self-limiting beliefs in order creatively to develop previously unrecognised qualities in ourselves. Jung likens this stage of the therapeutic process to the alchemy of *Nigredo* in which the alchemist breaks down the elements prior to their transformation, a vital step that precedes the generation of all new forms.

The Empty-Centre

Jung associated the darkness of *Nigredo* with the 'shadow side' of our unconscious, the negative traits we project onto others as well as our dreams. Rooted in our instinctual nature, this shadow side, when unacknowledged, can erupt from the unconscious with destructive force,[70] fixating in the form of a projection on anything perceived as a threat, whether an individual, a community, nation, or even darkness itself.

During a crisis, like the Covid-19 pandemic, we are especially vulnerable to shadow projections, either casting our 'shadow' on others, or carrying the shadow put on us by others. Yet, when we recognise our own shadow as part of ourselves, admitting our fallibilities, fears and prejudices and taking responsibility for our actions instead of blaming others, we can withdraw our projections.

When we are clear about what is 'ours', it also becomes possible to disengage from the projections of others, calmly returning the problem to its 'owner'. This withdrawal of projections, both our own and from others, frees up the energies caught in the negative dynamic and opens the way to creative life changes.

Our collective human participation in the shadow is expressed in symbolic language that reaches beyond individual birth and death and constellates what Jung called an 'archetype'. As Jung explained, 'The archetype is, so to speak, an "eternal" presence and the only question is whether it is perceived by the conscious mind or not.'[71] For example, the archetypal *sol niger* has a heavy darkness, associated with 'shadow' attributes: fearfulness, depression and death. An alchemical emblem from the 16th-century work *The Splendor Solis* (Figure 6), powerfully depicts the *sol niger* of *Nigredo*.[72] Fittingly, Sufis call this oppressive darkness 'captive light', an apt description for how our shadow projections can entrap us, keeping us from seeing the light in the darkness.

Jung taught that by making the darkness in ourselves conscious, we become enlightened, being liberated from the ego's domination. This involves a confrontation with what Jung referred to in correspondence as the 'empty-centre' within each of us.[73] He writes: 'Emptiness in this sense doesn't mean "absence" or "vacancy," but something unknowable which is endowed with highest intensity.' He further explains that the term 'centre' could be described more generally as 'God'

Figure 6. The *Sol Niger* of *Nigredo*

or, more specifically, as the 'God-image' or as the supreme archetype of the Self.[74] He notes that archetypes can only point the way to the 'empty-centre' — they help us to name and conceptualise, yet the 'empty-centre' can never be fully known.[75] In Jung's view, the more we become conscious of our own shadow, the more whole we become, and the closer we move towards the centre.

The Jungian analyst Edward Edinger shares a dream of his own in which the empty-centre appeared.[76] He saw a one-celled organism, like an amoeba, that had, instead of a nucleus, a large empty hole through which the blue sky shone. Edinger described this hole as 'a window that looks out on another dimension of reality'.[77] As he explains, most of the time we rush to fill the 'emptiness' of the centre with a culture-bound God-image. Or we may project our shadow onto the centre, not only our existential fears, but also painful feelings like loneliness and despair.

That is why learning to 'sit with' difficult feelings in waking life, owning them and working through them therapeutically, helps prepare us for an encounter with the 'empty-centre' in both the visible world and dreams. (I recall an early lucid dream in which the entire dreamscape gave way to what felt like 'the empty-centre', a still and silent void, causing me to fear that I may have died.)

After many lucid dreams, I began to understand that when I withdrew my projections and thereby acceded to the Greater Wisdom of spiritual insight, I found myself 'pulled' into the Black Light that illuminates the 'empty-centre', learning over time to become peacefully at one with this infinite, radiant darkness.

In lucidity, as we regain the capacity for self-reflection, we also retain our connections to the deep feelings aroused in the dreaming state. In this way, lucid dreaming has the potential to bring focused thinking and emotional intelligence together. Whereas Jung applied the alchemical model to understanding psycho-spiritual growth expressed through dream imagery, I have found that similar stages can also be *consciously* initiated in a lucid dream to powerful therapeutic effect. For example, in the following dream, as I am able to withdraw my projections, my personal psychology is transcended, opening the door to the Greater Wisdom:

I am in the home of a man with whom I had an affair during a lonely time in my first marriage. He wants to take me in his arms. A part of my mind resists, for we have ended our relationship, but then, bowing my head, I give in to an overwhelming desire. In that moment, I remember bowing my head in the Sufi meditation on the word 'Mabud', Arabic for 'lover', and recall that the word refers to the Beloved aspect of the Divine. With this memory, I realise I am dreaming and that my real longing is for the Divine.

Dramatically, the entire dreamscape gives way to Black Light, filled with an ethereal and exquisitely beautiful music. I have no thoughts as I take in the quality of the Black Light. After some time, although without a visible dream body, I feel that my subtle hands are illuminated with energy of the Spirit. I awake, feeling the soft and holy darkness around me.

Subsequently, I was to discover that Black Light, when freed of all projections, pulses with an all-encompassing, soulful intelligence, from which living light forms arise, alive with the beauty, intelligence and dynamism of Spirit. The forms that this light takes may depend on the individual soul-longing of the dreamer.

In my experience, revelatory light forms have imparted qualities of mind, soul and spirit, fulfilling my soul's desire to be known, to be loved and to love. At the same time, I am aware of the desire of Spirit for the same. I will be discussing these living light forms further in the following two chapters, but before doing so, I would like to share with you two more encounters with Black Light in Lucid Surrender.

The Alchemy of Lucid Surrender

Let us look more closely at what may follow the cessation of more familiar dream imagery when Lucid Surrender takes place.

We might begin by asking ourselves what we habitually project onto the colour black in waking life, as, for example, when we are alone in the dark. If you had to walk down an unfamiliar city street at night, how would you feel? Safe or under threat? If the latter, what perceived threats might you fear the darkness hides? How does this fear change your experience? If you met a stranger in the darkness, especially if that person was of a different gender, culture or ethnicity to you, how would you feel then?

Similarly, when in a lucid dream, projecting our shadow into the darkness of the Black Light can bring overpowering fear, confusion, disappointment, emptiness, loneliness, despair, shame, guilt or anger. Worse still, the disappearance of the dream narrative, along with our dream body, can feel like a terrifying annihilation.

The Hindu goddess Kali, the black goddess called 'the Destroyer', symbolically represents this aspect of darkness. Yet, she is also known as 'the Transformer' because in liberating her followers from the constraints of the ego, she returns all to its primordial unity. In the *Mahanirvana Tantra*, it is written:

> Just as all colours disappear in black,
> So all names and forms disappear in her.[78]

In lucidity, I find that when I project my fears into the darkness, the Black Light assumes strong 'Kali' attributes. At such moments, I fear the unknown. However, if I am able to calm my fears by drawing on divine grace through breath, prayer and song, then the way opens to Lucid Surrender, as the following dream excerpt shows:

I walk in a field as a strong wind comes up and pulls at me. I resist the wind even as it blows the very dreamscape away. I have difficulty becoming fully lucid as the Black Light and winds carry me down into a darkness that I perceive as evil. Ghostly beings of ashen white appear, wailing and gnashing their teeth like in the biblical descriptions of hell. My heart goes out to them. I fear I am being taken to the very bowels of hell. So I begin to pray. At this moment, I recognise the wind as Spirit and wonder if the ghost-like beings are from the hell my own mind has made. I continue to pray as I yield to the Black Light.

In this dream, I am eventually able to see the hellish shadow for what it is: a projection of my own mind. My prayerful attitude helps me to draw on the grace needed to move beyond these mental constructs.

In Lucid Surrender the dreamer must not only learn to withdraw their projections but also to restrain the ego's desire for control, for the aim is to accede one's personal will to the 'Highest Will'[79] — to yield to the Greater Wisdom[80] — a yielding known in the Taoist tradition as 'practising eternity'.[81]

We see this process in the following lucid dream when I acquiesce to the revelation of the Black Light:

I walk on a city street past a parking lot full of rubble, and I think, 'That's like my mind, and that's not how I want my mind to be.' Instantly, I become lucid and the dreamscape falls away into blackness. I am lifted up by surging winds at a tremendous speed into the powerful spaciousness of the Black Light. To maintain my focus, I sing a sacred song that arises spontaneously. After some while, my soul is suspended in an endless black space through which a delicate, yet forceful wind blows. The wind invigorates and fills me with a refined desire. I wait trustingly. Then I have the feeling that this vastness in which I rest is making love to me, as though my consciousness has become the strings of the Aeolian harp that send vibrations into my very being. Gently, this leads to a 'cosmic' ecstasy much finer and more ethereal than an ordinary orgasm. I wonder at how these vibrations move all of Creation and how Creation springs from a great love and joy and a desire for being.

I continue to rest in the Black Light until my being is

whisked onto the winds as if I am being carried on a powerful current. For once I don't feel at all afraid, just curious and not worried about 'getting back'.

This dream, ending as I awaken with these words ringing in my ear, 'The universe can make love to you!', has continued thereafter to enliven me, body and soul.

Life After Death

The 'death' brought about by the withdrawal of projections in Lucid Surrender brings to mind an alchemical emblem in J. D. Mylius's *Philosophia Reformata* (1622), featuring a skeleton standing on a flaming black sphere (Figure 7).[82] At first glance, the emblem looks rather frightening. It is, nonetheless, a pictorial drawing of inner transformation that applies both to Jung's alchemical model and to the alchemy of Lucid Surrender.

Figure 7. The *Nigredo* Standing on the *Rotundum*

Jung refers to this emblem as 'The *nigredo* standing on the *rotundum*', a spherical form of gold.[83] Drawing on my own learning, I would suggest that the 'rotundum' depicts an eclipsed or black sun, signifying that the energies of the shadow have become available for positive change through the withdrawal of projections. The resulting sense of inner alignment with the soul's nature is symbolised here by the two angelic presences.

To return to the dream of hellish projection I reported earlier:

Once I realise that the hell before me is a creation of my own mind, the winds on the Black Light carry me to a still place, where interlaced cubes of blue light radiate to infinity in a double-helix spiral. As I stand contemplating the light form, I feel that each cube constitutes a very basic building block of life, as well as representing every individual human life — all intertwined.

I know myself to be part of this chain of life. In that moment, I perceive the expansiveness of my vision and exhaustion of my actual earthly body. It seems strange to me that both are true and that this beautiful light form should require my limited, exhausted self in order to be known. It feels wondrous and very humbling, as well as inspiring and encouraging. After some time in this state, I awaken.

The practice of Lucid Surrender requires that we enter the Black Light with trust. There, we find unbounded Beingness, known over millennia to mystics and sages. It is the spacious and sentient 'naked awareness' revealed to Tibetan Buddhists,[84] the bliss referred to as *Sat Chit Ananda* in the Vedas, and in Taoism, the 'Limitless Infinite' that gives birth to 'the ten thousand things'.[85]

Importantly, Christian mysticism distinguishes between the darkness that is associated with the 'fallen' state of matter, the Lesser Wisdom, and the darkness that reveals the Greater Wisdom. The early Christian mystic Dionysius the Areopagite tells us: 'For by the resistless and absolute ecstasy in all purity, from thyself and all, thou wilt be carried on high, to the super-essential ray of the Divine darkness, when thou hast cast all away and is free from all.'[86] Elsewhere, in his poem 'Dark Night', St John of the Cross writes:

> Oh Night, my guide!
> Oh Night, more loving than dawn!
> Oh Night you join
> Beloved to Beloved,
> Oneness transformed![87]

Over time, I have learned to trust the luminous darkness as the spaciousness where Spirit abides and to approach it with a humble mind and heart. I have learned to wait patiently as sacred living lights appear, illumined intelligences of goodness, beauty and truth, divine emanations of that 'infinite sphere, the centre of which is everywhere and the circumference nowhere.'[88]

Notes:

59. First published in the International Association for the Studies of Dreams, *DreamTime Magazine* (March 2012), as 'The Alchemy and Archetype of Black Light in Lucid Surrender', this revised chapter reflects the learning gained subsequently from hundreds of lucid dreams.
60. Originally from Sir George Ripley's *Compound of Alchymie in Ripley Reviv'd*, Eirenaeus Philalethes (William Cooper) 1668-1688, 357. Early English Books Online Text Creation Partnership, 2011, https://quod.lib.umich.edu/e/eebo/A61326.0001.001/1:13.5?rgn=div2;view=fulltext
61. Based on the physics experiment entitled 'Project Eureka' as described by Arthur Zajonc in his *Catching the Light: The Entwined History of Light and Mind* (New York and Oxford: Oxford University Press, 1993), 1–2.
62. See the NASA article 'Dark Energy, Dark Matter,' accessed 10 July 2020, https://science.nasa.gov/astrophysics/focus-areas/what-is-dark-energy
63. The full verse from the 'Emerald Tablet' is translated by Robert Steele and Dorothea Waley Singer in 'The Emerald Table' as 'True it is, without falsehood most certain and true. That which is above is like to that which is below, and that which is below is like to that which is above, to accomplish the miracle of the one thing.' See Proceedings of the Royal Society of Medicine, 21, No. 3 (January 1928): 485–501,
https://www.ncbi.nlm.nih.gov/pmc/articles/PMC2101974/?page=1
64. Michael Sendivogius, *The New Chemical Light. Second part. Concerning Sulphur*, ed. Jean Pierre Donabin (originally published by J. Elliot and Co., London, 1893), 138, http://www.livres-d-hermes.com/PDF/NEWCH101.PDF
65. Ibid.
66. For a groundbreaking study of the psycho-spiritual understanding of darkness, see Stanton Marlan's *The Black Sun: The Alchemy and Art of Darkness* (Texas: A & M University Press, 2005).
67. Mahmud Shabistari, *The Garden of Mystery*, trans. Robert Abdul Hayy Darr (Cambridge: Cherwynd House, 2007), 46, verses 123 and 128.
68. See Henry Corbin's *The Man of Light in Iranian Sufism* in which he presents Sufi teachings on the mystical encounter with luminous darkness and coloured lights. (Omega Publications: New Lebanon, New York, 1994), 100.
69. Ibid., 116.
70. Carl Gustav Jung, 'The Shadow', in *The Collected Works of C.G. Jung: Psychology and Alchemy*, Vol. 9ii, trans. R. F. C. Hull, Herbert Read, Michael Fordham, eds. Gerhard Adler and William McGuire (London: Routledge & Kegan Paul, 1953, 1974), paras. 13–19.
71. Jung, *The Collected Works*, Vol. 12, 'The Symbolism of the Mandala', para. 329.

72. This depiction comes from Salomon Tismosin's 'Splendor Solis'. https://wellcomecollection.org/works/xrvf3w96?wellcomeImagesUrl=/indexplus/image/V0025641.html, Attribution 4.0 International (CC BY 4.0). To learn more about this emblem, see Joseph L. Henderson and Dyane N. Sherwood, *Transformation of the Psyche: The Symbolic Alchemy of the Splendor Solis* (London and New York: Routledge Taylor & Francis Group, 2005).
73. 'Letter to Pastor Bernett', 13 June 1955, in *C. G. Jung's Letters: Volume 2, 1951-1961*, ed. Gerhard Adler in collaboration with Aniela Jaffé, trans. R. F. C Hull (London: Routledge & Kegan Paul, 1976), 257-264.
74. Ibid.
75. Ibid.
76. Cited in Edward F. Edinger's *The New God Image: A Study of Jung's Key Letters Concerning the Evolution of the Western God-Image*, eds. D. D. Cordic and C. Yates, (Wilmette, IL: Chiron Publications, 1996), 22.
77. Ibid., 22.
78. From Chapter 13, 'Installation of the Devata', verse 5, in the *Mahanirvana Upanishad (Tantra of the Great Liberation)*, as translated by Ajit Mookerjee in her *Kali: The Feminine Force* (London: Thames & Hudson, Ltd., 1988), 62. See also Arthur Avalon's and John George Woodruffe's translation: 'As white, yellow, and other colours all disappear in black, in the same way, O Shailaja! all beings enter Kali', 157, http://public-library.uk/ebooks/59/94.pdf
79. Assagioli, *The Act of Will*, 106-122.
80. See Chapter Nine on nightmares and Chapter Ten on lucid dreaming in my *The Hidden Lives of Dreams* (London: Bonnier Books UK, 2020).
81. Mitchell, *Tao Te Ching*, No. 52.
82. Engraving by Balthazar Schwan, 1622
83. Jung, *The Collected Works*, Vol. 12, 88. Illustration No. 34, 'The *Nigredo* Standing on the *Rotundum*'.
84. See Tenzin Rinpoche Wangyal, *Awakening the Luminous Mind: Tibetan Meditation for Inner Peace and Joy*, ed. Marcy Vaughn (London: Hay House, Inc., 2012).
85. Referred to as *Wuji*.
86. See *The Collected Works of Dionysius the Aeropagite*, ed. Anthony Uyl, trans. Rev. John Parker (Ontario, Canada: Solace Games, 2015), 52.
87. From the poem 'Dark Night' by St John of the Cross, written in 1578. This is my own translation from the Spanish.
88. This idea appears in a medieval teaching, most likely from Rabbinical sources, that describes 'God' as a being whose centre is everywhere and circumference nowhere.

Chapter 7

THE SPIRITUAL ALCHEMY OF LIGHT WITHIN DARKNESS[89]

They discover that in the very darkness of nature a light is hidden, a little spark without which the darkness would not be darkness.[90]

— C. G. Jung

What kind of light illuminates our dreams? Across the universe, the full electro-magnetic spectrum — of which visible light represents only a small fraction — extends to invisible wavelengths that vibrate at increasingly higher frequencies, from radio waves, microwaves, infrared and ultraviolet radiation, to X-rays and gamma rays. Understood in this way, visible and invisible wavelengths across the electromagnetic spectrum have many functions. For example, light wavelengths create heat, warming us and imparting life; surgeons use laser light to perform operations; fibre-optics transmit information, enabling near-instantaneous communication; infrared telescopes allow astrophysicists to peer through interstellar dust; X-rays penetrate soft tissue to reveal bone; and electron microscopes image molecular structures.

Analogously, the inner light of dreams extends to a spectrum of *visible* and *invisible* wavelengths. Just as the light of day bestows life and with it the visible perceptual world, so the inner light of dreams reveals not only images but also illuminates an inner world of thought and feeling that renews us nightly.

Medieval alchemists understood the inner light of the mind to be composed of *scintillae* or sparks from the animating principle of the 'world soul', which they viewed as akin to the Holy Spirit. They called this light the *lumen naturae*, the inner light of Nature, one that imparts wisdom and serves as the guiding 'star' in each one of us;[91] it is as Jung explains, 'the light of the darkness itself'.[92] Furthermore, the great physician and alchemist Paracelsus tells us that we learn of the light of Nature through our dreams.[93]

The Alchemy of The Inner Light

In following the injunction to 'Awake in Sleep!', alchemists made conscious use of alchemical emblems to illustrate processes associated with both the physical and inner light.[94] Using visual imagery, they encoded light's esoteric mysteries in their alchemical emblems. The 'Subtle Art of Alchemy' tracked not only chemical processes but also a profound spiritual alchemy, that of the inner light's transformative power.

The 17th-century alchemical emblem entitled 'The Great Work', which was introduced in Chapter Five, can be viewed as illustrating alchemical teachings on the inner light. The emblem displays four spheres stacked vertically: ascending, the orbs are associated with the alchemical colours black, white, yellow and red.

These luminous spheres represent a sequence of transformational processes. In the practice of chemical alchemy, they followed the operation of sublimation wherein the black sphere signifies the transformation of solid to liquid; the white from liquid to gas; the gold from gas to the 'quintessence'; and the red the return to matter. These four spheres illustrate the spiritualisation of matter and the materialisation of Spirit in four overlapping stages, *Nigredo*, *Albedo*, *Citrinitas* and *Rubedo*.

Jung viewed these four stages and the colours representing them from both a psychological and spiritual perspective, identifying the black with the breaking down of our ego-based identity, the white with the emergence of the individual soul nature, the gold with the aligning of our soul with the greater Transpersonal Will, and the red with manifesting our human spiritual potential in life. In my experience, these alchemical colours, when they appear in dreams, both signpost and facilitate the dreamer's psycho-spiritual development, especially so in the lucid state.[95]

In the previous chapter, we took an in-depth look at the phenomenon of Black Light in Lucid Surrender. We explored how, when our minds are still and our hearts are open, the darkness of *Nigredo*, freed from psychological projections, becomes a glowing blackness, beyond space and time, alive with profound intelligence, full of joy and love.

Yet, paradoxically, Black Light first must initiate an 'ego-death', a breaking down of our usual sense of self. We find the parallel in medieval alchemy with the dissolution of matter into its basic properties, known as a *Mortificatio* (from the

Latin: *death*), which is necessary before chemical elements can be combined into new compounds. As earlier described, in this stage of Lucid Surrender, the dream world as we know it dissolves away, along with all points of reference by which we orientate our bodily sense of self. If we resist the disorientation caused by this loss, the encounter with darkness can feel like an annihilation, yet if we can trust and allow the dream to unfold, keeping our focus on the Highest Will, the dissolution leads to a profound perception of our subtle body in ecstatic union with the oneness of Spirit.

Alchemists used the images of the sexual union to describe the merging of opposites as two become one. We see this depicted in a 17th-century version of an alchemical manuscript called *The Pretiosissimum Donum Dei*, 'The Most Precious Gift of God'. [96] In illustrating the alchemical stages, the text draws on two key alchemical symbols: that of the flask (the container for 'The Great Work' of alchemy); and of the royal couple, the King and Queen, who embody the unification of sun and moon, mind and matter, Soul and Spirit.

An evocative emblem from this series shows the royal pair as lovers, joined in sexual union, while suspended in the blackness of the alchemical flask (Figure 8). Naked, the King and Queen become one, as they symbolically leave their identities behind. Similarly, in Lucid Surrender, the separative nature of the egoic self dissolves in the Black Light of *Nigredo*, preparing the dreamer for *Albedo*. This process has been described in a text written by a medieval alchemist:

And thus by the Gate of blackness thou must come in
To the light of Paradise in whiteness, if thou wilt win.⁹⁷

Figure 8. The Alchemical Flask — *Nigredo*

Albedo, The Whitening

Alchemists referred to the stage of *Albedo* or *the Whitening* as the white rose of alchemy. Notably, the transformation of the moon from darkness to fullness was understood to express the emergence of the soul's full potential. In the alchemical flask shown here (Figure 9), it is the Queen herself, dressed in white, who, kneeling, epitomises the white rose of *Albedo*:

Figure 9. The Alchemical Flask — *Albedo*

In the context of Lucid Surrender, I view the opening of this 'white rose' as a symbol for the soulful light forms that emerge from the Black Light. In *Albedo*, the alchemical 'light of grace',[98] the light of Soul imparts deeply felt realisations about our true nature. The following lucid dream is suffused with such 'whitening':

In lucidity, I find myself taken into the black, ecstatic light. Diaphanous veils of white begin to appear and disappear as if white sands spiral in the wind. My mind tries to make sense of what is happening, and I wonder if the sand blows off from the surface of the moon (even though I know this isn't possible). It is lovely to think that like the moon I am reflecting the sun's light to earth, as the individual soul is likewise illuminated by Spirit.

Although *Albedo* has associations with the soulfulness of moonlight, alchemists also described this stage as 'the peacock's tail', referring to the striking hues that appeared in the black oils of heated elements.[99] An alchemical emblem from the 16th-century *Splendor Solis* shows a peacock in a flask set against a dark backdrop. The peacock's tail beautifully symbolises the expansion of consciousness that arises from a profound encounter with coloured light forms, revealed in the following lucid dream:

I talk with a man in a garden. Looking around, I notice that there aren't many flowers, so I think: 'Let there be flowers.' When flowers don't appear, I am surprised because, after all, this is a dream. With this awareness, full lucidity comes as the dreamscape disappears and my being is carried by very hard and fast winds on the Black Light, leaving me breathless.

After a stunning downward movement through the Black Light, my invisible feet gently touch the ground. The sensation feels indescribably lovely, as if I have been lovingly set down on a soft forest floor that communicates with my soul. On the black incandescent expanse, there appears a large blue circle of light.

The circle reminds me of a fountain's base but without a central column. As I wait, cylindrical shafts of brilliant blue shoot up from the circle's centre. These turn to green as they break into a million shining drops of light. The green drops wash through my being like a blessing. I desire to weep tears for the beauty, for the unspoken knowing communicated in the green. It seems a shame to be alone in this experience. If only others could share in it! I feel a yearning to share the green.

With deepening lucidity, the expansion of consciousness is characterised by the emergence of increasingly beautiful, multi-dimensional forms of light.[100] Simple, two-dimensional shapes develop into three-dimensional forms suggestive of an inner capacity to hold paradoxical positions and reconcile opposites. While this progression occurs in non-lucid and lucid dreams, in the realm of lucidity, the geometric forms may become pivotal, taking on extensive proportions and relational resonances, and inviting us to participate in new ways of knowing and new qualities of being.

As I have found, forms reminiscent of Platonic solids have also expressed their own 'attunement'. In one dream my being is taken into the centre of a large dodecahedron alive with the chorus, 'Holy, holy, holy Lord, God of Power and Might, Heaven and Earth are full of your glory. Hosanna in the highest. Blessed is he who comes in the name of the Lord.'

In *Albedo*, radiant crystalline shapes emerge, enlarging the dreamer's capacity to bring the inner light into the outer world in multi-faceted ways, as in this dream:

A large painting of a mandala with a black surround and white centre hangs on a wall opposite me. A lovely woman stands to the right of the painting. She intends the artwork as a gift for me.

Looking at the mandala, I realise it represents the spiritual nature of lucidity. I also understand that this image is connected to my third eye or inner eye. With this, I become lucid. The dreamscape falls away and the white circle becomes a large twelve-sided emerald surrounded by blackness. I have the strange feeling that this precious stone has lodged between my brows. Thinking about this, I slowly come into waking consciousness.

Such light forms impart a soulful sense of inner harmony and heart-centred responsiveness, imbuing the dreamer with an intuitive understanding of their soul's nature and purpose. The delicate alchemy of *Albedo* in Lucid Surrender prepares the soul to receive the light of Spirit, bestowed by the golden sphere of *Citrinitas*.

Citrinitas, The Yellowing

Citrinitas corresponds to the celestial realm, where the conjoining of Soul and Spirit takes place. Alchemists describe the unitive experience of *Citrinitas* as the alchemical *coniunctio*, symbolised by the royal couple, the King and Queen, imparting a deep sense of oneness with the Divine. Here, we discover our 'inner gold', described by the Jungian analyst Robert Johnson as: 'the highest value in the human psyche.... When I speak about gold this way, I am also speaking about God. These are two ways to describe the mystery.'[101]

In *Citrinitas* imagery, the colour gold takes various forms that represent the inherent unity and eternal nature of the suprasensible world. The alchemical flask shown here, from the medieval alchemical manuscript the *Cabala Mineralis*,[102] portrays the staff of caduceus, the symbol of Hermes Trismegistus, legendary sage, healer and alchemist, also known as Mercury, set in a field of green and gold (Figure 10).

Figure 10. The Alchemical Flask — *Citrinitas*

During *Citrinitas*, limitless light forms in vibrant colours further expand our consciousness so that we know our individual nature to be part of an infinitely greater whole, as this dream illustrates:

A friend from childhood rests with me on the floor of the bedroom I had when I was five. To my astonishment a rattle-

snake appears between us and glides over towards me. I know that I am dreaming and that the snake won't harm me. It lifts its head and licks at the air around my legs. Gliding past me, it disappears into the darkness on the other side. I am curious about what this portends.

With this thought, my soul lifts out of my body. Great joy seizes me as the dreamscape gives way to the Black Light. The ecstasy is intense and the winds powerful, making it hard to focus. Reassuringly, a holy song arises in my soul. When the movement ceases, I find myself lying on golden sands. I stand up and 'water' laps around my feet. It's then I become aware of a sea of Black Light before me. Lacy patterns of golden light move on the surface of the darkly shining 'waters' like sea foam. Briefly, I fear I may be swallowed up by this sea and lost, but then a voice says clearly and beautifully, 'Come and wash in my love.' All fear dissolves, and I rush into the resplendent black waters.

As I experienced in this dream, Citrinitas light forms enfold the dreamer in unconditional love, a profound sense of oneness, infusing the qualities needed to manifest the gifts of the Soul and Spirit in waking life. In the words of St John of the Cross, 'The soul shines with the light of love' in 'shining transparencies'.[103]

Six years into lucid dreaming, I had a series of *Citrinitas* dreams that completely shattered my preconceptions of the Divine, exceeding anything I could have imagined in their beauty and power, and culminating in the next dream of 'The Golden Cloud':

I wake up around 4.30 a.m. Spontaneously, a sacred song rises up in my mind. As I sing, silently repeating the song with the breath, a whirring sound around my head starts up and I enter lucidity. For some time, my being hovers suspended in an intermediary space of Black Light, tugged at by an unseen strong current. I call out, 'Take me to you, Lord!', and my soul is released onto the rushing Black Light.

I see before me a new light structure, a V-shape of blue and white effervescent light lit up like a sparkler on New Year's Eve. As I approach this vortex of light, I feel unsure of what to do with my invisible arms, whether to open them to the light or bring my hands together in prayer. A voice says, 'Just be,' so I remain still while carried on the winds. Spontaneously, the Lord's Prayer bubbles up inside me as I burst into a realm of gold.

The golden radiance has unusual dimensions, akin to being inside a limitless piece of amber. In the distance, I see an immense golden cloud, the richness of which stands out even against the backdrop of gold. The cloud hovers over the horizon expectantly. I know it is the Lord, and my heart leaps up. Two towering silhouetted angelic guardians open a gate to a golden path between them. The Holy winds carry my soul through innumerable worshipful shadows ever nearer to the golden cloud.

Approaching the cloud, I become aware of an achingly beautiful piece of music. It feels both unknown to me and yet strangely familiar, full of layered harmonies and motifs. Nothing I have ever heard before shares its texture or depth, as the music seemingly arises from the very fabric of the space and golden light around me. I am surrounded by a perfect balance of paradoxical qualities: tremendous power and petal-soft tenderness, simplicity and profundity, mercy and might, justice and compassion, longing and fulfilment, immanence and transcendence. But the dominant quality within this golden cloud feels like a mysterious beauty and richness, in the folds of which rests deep humility, as in the petals of a rose. Suddenly, I realise that music sounds like a variation of a tune I sing to the Lord's Prayer while I am praying. I wonder if the Spirit hears my simple rendition this way. I am filled with the desire to create a musical score so that others can share in this rendition of the prayer, but since I lack the ability to do that, it strikes me that I'll just have to bring this music into life through my actions. The music accompanies me back towards waking consciousness.

In this dream, it felt that my inner alignment with the Highest Will enabled a reciprocity between myself and the Golden Cloud. As Johnson has pointed out, gold, while symbolising the eternal, nevertheless has a relational quality that we can mould and shape.[104] The light of *Citrinitas* helps us to reclaim our 'inner gold' and to prepare us for the re-shaping of our lives, in the fourth and final alchemical stage — the red sphere of *Rubedo*.

Rubedo, The Reddening

Alchemists referred to immersion in the light of *Citrinitas* as 'the Heavenly tincture'.[105] This 'tincture' was to be brought into earthly existence through the fourth alchemical process, known as *Rubedo*. The *Donum Dei* depicts *Rubedo* as the King, dressed in gold, standing boldly within a flask of the precious red elixir (Figure 11).

Figure 11. The Alchemical Flask — *Rubedo*

The alchemists sought to create a physical elixir that would confer immortality. In Lucid Surrender, *Rubedo* brings new, light-given capacities and learning from our dreams into manifestation in the physical world — the bringing of Spirit into matter.

The realisation of a dream can take many forms and may span many years. In my own life, I had already been working with dreams and writing about them for more than ten years, but I still had much to learn from my dreams and from life before I was ready to embark on my books. Then, in 2017, I had a dream in which a colleague of mine, a well-known lucid dreamer, appeared, reminding me that I must get my learning from the dreams 'out there' in published form. Not long after, I was unexpectedly commissioned by Bonnier Books to write *The Hidden Lives of Dreams*.

I felt unsure about writing a book on dreams at a time when the world was facing so many environmental and social crises, until I had the following lucid dream:

During my prayers, I drift off and find myself on the Black Light, filled with ecstasy.

Before me, I see the illuminated entry to a long tunnel. After going through this, I overlook an ocean of breath-taking stars surrounding an Earth-like planet. Coming closer, I can see towering mountain peaks for hundreds of miles in every direction, yet, in spite of their great height, no snow covers the mountain ranges.

Then I am taken to a higher elevation from where I can see large patches of brownish grey covering the planet. I am saddened to realise that this is pollution from sprawling cities.

Intuitively, I am given to understand that this planet is experiencing disastrous climate change! I feel deeply grieved for it. I wonder if it is Earth. 'How' I ask, 'can I help? How can I let people know?' The answer comes: Through the way I present Earth's beauty and plight in my writing on dreams!

The next day, I begin to weave this theme into *The Hidden Lives of Dreams*, and directly after publication, I turned to writing this book on Lucid Surrender.

Like me, you can also look to your dreams for the infusion of creative energy and spiritual willpower needed to bring your soul's purpose to life. As we engage with our dreams, we can be inspired to express our heart's innermost desire fully in the world, like the alchemical rose, rooted in the darkness and blossoming in the light.

Notes:

89. Originally published in *DreamTime Magazine, IASD* (September 2011) as 'The Spiritual Alchemy of Black Light'. This paper has been heavily revised.
90. Jung, *The Collected Works*, Vol. 13, para. 197.
91. See Carl Jung's summary of the alchemical understanding of the *lumen naturae* in his *Collected Works*, Vol. 8, pars. 388–396 and in his Vol. 13, 'The Light of The Darkness', paras. 197–199.
92. Jung, *The Collected Works*, Vol. 13, para. 197.
93. Ibid., para. 391. Jung cites this particular teaching from the *Liber de Caducis* by Paracelsus.
94. For a fascinating study of this premise, see Urszula Szulakowska's *The Alchemy of Light: Geometry and Optics in Late Renaissance Alchemical Illustration* (Boston, Massachusetts: Brill, 2000).
95. For a detailed analysis of alchemical colours and symbols in dreams, see Nigel Hamilton's *Awakening Through Dreams: The Journey Through the Inner Landscape* (London: Karnac Books, 2014).
96. The earliest edition of this work is from the 15th-century work and is attributed to Georgius Aurach de Argentina, also known as 'Anrach'. This 17th century version is held in the Paris, Bibliothèque L'Arsenal MS. 975 (90 C.S.A.L.) posted on Adam McLean's website https://www.alchemywebsite.com/Emblems_manuscripts_Donum_Dei_Arsenal.html. See also Alexander Roob's *The Hermetic Museum: Alchemy & Mysticism* (Köln: TASCHEN GmbH, 2006), 358–363.
97. Ripley, *Compound of Alchymie*, 347.
98. Adam McLean, *The Alchemical Mandala: A Survey of the Mandala in the Western Esoteric Tradition* (Phanes Press: Grand Rapids, MI, 2002), 124.
99. Stanislas Klossowski de Rola, *Alchemy: The Secret Art* (London: Thames & Hudson Ltd., 1973, 1997), 217.
100. Nigel Hamilton, 'Dreams of Awakening' (IASD Conference presentation, Berkeley, 2012).
101. Robert Johnson, *Inner Gold: Understanding Psychological Projection* (Kilhei Hawaii: Koa Books, 2008), 3.
102. Attributed to Rabbi Simeon ben Cantara. See http://www.esolibri.it

103. See his commentary on 'Love's Living Flame: The Soul as Living Flame', *St John of the Cross*, 229.
104. Ibid., 5. Johnson's quote reads, 'Diamonds are the hardest matter on earth — unearthly, celestial, and impersonal. Gold is much softer, a matter of relationship, the Self as related.'
105. Adam McLean, *The Alchemical Mandala*, 80.

Chapter 8

Lucid Surrender and the Alchemical *Coniunctio*: A Post-Jungian Approach[106]

> *The quintessence is that which is extracted from a substance — From all plants and from everything that has life — then freed of all impurities and perishable parts, refined into highest purity and separated from all elements...* [107]
>
> — Paracelsus (Medieval physician and alchemist)

In the Middle Ages, alchemists, intrigued to discover that it takes 800 pounds of rose petals to create one pound of rose-scented concentrate, concluded that a person's soul could likewise be distilled into an essence suggestive of their essential nature — the fragrance of the soul. In the process of breaking down substances into oils, they undertook the sacred art of making 'the fixed volatile and the volatile fixed', of transforming matter into Spirit and freeing the Spirit in matter. The art of perfumery provided alchemists with an apt metaphor for describing correspondences between physical process and spiritual alchemy, the process of 'Soul making'.[108]

The alchemy of perfumery can be broadly grouped into four stages: separate, dissolve, recombine and fix. Firstly, separate the rose petals from the stem. Secondly, dissolve the petals through distillation by heating them in a solution to extract the flower's essence. Thirdly, recombine the extracted essence with another to create a new scent; and, finally, fix the perfume's ephemeral fragrance. [109]

As Jung points out, psycho-spiritual development mirrors these stages. He observes, 'Alchemy describes, not merely in general outline but often in the most astonishing detail, the same psychological phenomenology which can be observed in the analysis of unconscious processes.' [110] According to Jung's alchemical model, we must first separate out our conditioning, complexes and cultural patterns from our unconscious identification with the world around us. This involves a dissolving of the ego initiated by a life situation, such as a crisis of loss or love to which the ego must accept. The shattering emotional power of such experiences breaks down the ego and opens the heart, helping us to become more conscious of who we truly are.

We then must reintegrate this new knowledge, expanding our sense of self and our worldview. Ultimately, this process will be 'fixed' in life through transformative action in the waking world. [111] Alchemically speaking, the re-integration of opposing elements to form a new substance is described as the inner 'marriage', a *coniunctio* that heralds the King and Queen, also known as *Sol* and *Luna*, as the royal couple.

A series of emblems from a collection of twenty woodcuts known as the *Rosarium Philosophorum* (1550), [112] *The Rosary of the Philosophers*, features the alchemical King and Queen, conveying through images the unfolding of this psycho-spiritual transformation. The *Rosarium* emblems can be divided into two sets representing the four alchemical stages, the first set illustrative of *Nigredo* and *Albedo*, the second of *Citrinitas* and *Rubedo*, each emblem, like a bead on a rosary, invoking a sacred reflection.

Jung, in 'The Psychology of the Transference',[113] elaborates on eleven of the illustrations in this series, viewing the royal marriage as a mirror of the union between ego-consciousness and the soul. He notes, 'The alchemical image of the *coniunctio*... plays the same role in the exploration of the darkness of the psyche [the unconscious] as it played in the investigation of the riddle of matter.'[114]

Whereas Jung primarily focuses on eleven emblems from the first half of the *Rosarium* sequence, which includes lunar imagery representative of *Albedo*, in this chapter, I shall take into account seven additional emblems that represent the solar imagery of *Citrinitas* and *Rubedo*, thereby expanding on Jung's earlier premise.

The 'marriage' between two substances or 'bodies' can be viewed as producing a new state on three levels of alchemy: physical, psychological and spiritual alchemy. On the physical level, such as in the alchemy of perfumery, this involves two elements combining through the alchemical process of *solve et coagula* — 'dissolve and coagulate', describing the breaking down of matter and the creation of a new substance.

In archetypal psychology, this marriage between two 'bodies' is personified by the Royal couple, the King and the Queen. The King, typically pictured standing under the sun, the aegis of Spirit, embodies the purified ego-principle of action, while the Queen, under the moon, embodies Soul, providing intuitive wisdom. In transpersonal psychotherapy, the relationship between the King and Queen corresponds to the integration of the ego and the soul that takes place as a person becomes more conscious of the unconscious dynamics that had previously blocked their personal growth.

Through the lens of spiritual alchemy, the King and Queen represent the exoteric and esoteric realms respectively. The King signifies the visible physical world; the Queen the invisible, subtle spiritual realm. The King requires the Queen to give meaning and depth to his active principle, whereas the Queen requires an active principle to bring her subtle essence, the soul's creative imagination, into manifestation.

My own understanding of the *Rosarium* series is based on the psycho-spiritual processes that I have undergone in lucid dreaming through the practice of Lucid Surrender. Here, the 'alchemical vessel', where psycho-spiritual transformation takes place, occurs within the conscious dreaming of Lucid Surrender. I aim to show how the archetypal narrative of the *Rosarium* finds expression in Lucid Surrender.

The *Rosarium* begins with the image of a fountain (Figure 12). The fountain portrays the ego's 'participation mystique',[115] our unconscious identification with cultural conditioning and the perceptual world. When we experience dreaming as a reality in which we are fully immersed, we are caught up in the illusion of the dream.

Figure 12. The Alchemical Fountain

The next emblem shows the King and Queen, *Sol* and *Luna*, separated yet joined by the criss-crossing blossoms they hold in their right hands and by touching their left hands. In addition to the four flowers, their separateness is reconciled by the presence of a dove bearing a fifth flower, which Jung views as the Holy Ghost descending from the 'quintessential star'[116] (Figure 13). With the onset of lucidity, we become aware that we are dreaming, and, to that extent, we have withdrawn our unconscious projections from the dream scene. The differentiation of dreamer and dream is mirrored in the duality of the royal couple.

Figure 13. The King and Queen

By invoking Lucid Surrender, the dreamer carries the withdrawal of projections further in surrendering the ego to the transpersonal — an indefinable mysterious and powerful Love at the heart of Creation, akin to the Holy Spirit, as I realised in the following dream:

> *I enter a garage full of wooden furniture, and I begin to think how it would fit in the centre where I work. Then I realise that I am dreaming and so bow my head, filled with joy. I am carried so fast and forcefully on the Black Light that I begin to feel frightened. I say, 'Well, I feel afraid, God, but that's just me with my fear.' To steady myself, I repeat a sacred name. Although I have no apparent physical body, I feel a strong desire to completely prostrate myself before the dark and divine*

immensity that I face. This happens with great force. My old self has no place here, as though it has shattered by the impact. After some time, a feeling of intense pleasure arises. I see a tiny form lying on a bed far below me. The figure looks so small I think that it must be a baby. As I am brought closer, I realise that the figure in the bed is me, lying there praying. For a still, breath-taking moment, I see myself through the loving eyes of the Holy Spirit, suffused with a touchingly beautiful innocence.

In lucidity, I have found that Lucid Surrender can be initiated through a gesture such as bowing my head, through words or simply by opening my mind and heart to curiosity and wonder. In this state, the everyday persona is stripped away, and we become 'naked' before a Greater Wisdom. Such nakedness also suggests an innocence and humility of spirit, qualities that confer protection upon the initiate.

We see this state pictured in the next emblem where the royal couple appears naked, having shed the garments of their personas in preparation for union (Figure 14).

Here, the King holds a banner reading, 'O *Luna*, be my wife', while the Queen's reads, 'O *Sol*, I submit to Thee.' In this context, submission refers to the soul's willingness to serve Spirit, the animating principle of life itself.

Figure 14. *Sol* and *Luna*

The initial stage of Lucid Surrender corresponds psycho-spiritually to the stage of *Nigredo*. In a lucid dream, this may involve the dreamscape dissolving into an apparent void, as the dreamer 'dies' to their ego. Yet, the dreamer can trust a timeless psycho-spiritual truth: when something dies, something new is born.

In Lucid Surrender, the loss of all that locates the waking world ego in time and space can lead to the sensation of a 'free-fall' in which there is an abrupt and dizzying descent, ending in a still, infinite space. The psyche is now prepared for a sacred, luminous encounter. This can be seen in the following alchemical emblem by the imagery of the disrobed King and Queen poised on the edge of a hexagonal bath (Figure 15). The fountain marks the entrance into the realm of what James Hillman, Jungian analyst and founder of archetypal psychology, refers to as 'Soul-making'.[117]

Figure 15. The Alchemical Bath

It is of note that, in Lucid Surrender, illuminated hexagons are sometimes woven into the fabric of the Black Light, as in this dream excerpt:

With lucidity, the dream falls away and my soul is carried a great distance into the Black Light. Eventually, I see patterns of light across the expanse of luminous blackness. Rows of crystal hexagonal structures like in a honeycomb with spaces in between form a wide tunnel. I descend at an incredible speed into this wormhole structure. Far away, at the tunnel's entrance, a speck of light shines. For a moment I am concerned that I have fallen into a deep well, until I recall that this is a lucid dream, and this forms a way to a new dimension.

In the alchemy of perfumery, droplets of the flower's essential oil condensing in the alchemical flask were taken to indicate the release of the 'etheric body'. Concerning its nature, Jung remarks, 'It is beyond our grasp *per* definition; the subtle body is a transcendental concept that cannot be expressed in terms of our language or philosophical views, because they are all inside categories of time and space.' [118] In the practice of Lucid Surrender, my etheric body either remains invisible or appears as light. Either way, the senses of sight, sound and touch feel heightened

The alchemists associated the release of this subtle body with the feeling of intense ecstasy, as depicted by the *Rosarium* emblem in which the royal couple float in ecstatic sexual union on the surface of the water (Figure 16) — the interface between the psyche and new dimensions of consciousness.

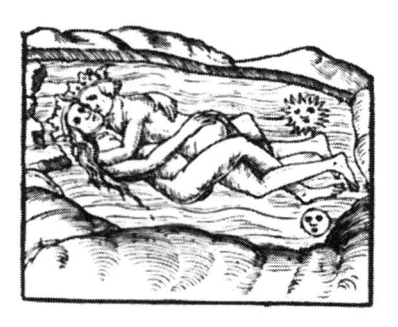

Figure 16. Ecstatic Union

If lucidity can be sustained through Lucid Surrender, the 'death' that follows incurs a profound loss of the mundane self, along with the expectations and beliefs associated with it.

In the *Rosarium*, this is illustrated in an emblem of the royal couple lying in a death-pose on a sepulchre, sharing one crown and one body (Figure 17). The hermaphroditic form reveals an inner unity that transcends all opposites.

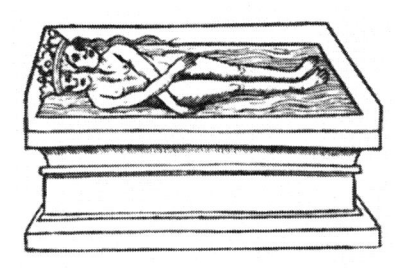

Figure 17. The Hermaphrodite on the Sepulchre

In the alchemical tradition, this merging of two purified bodies into one is required for the birth of the 'divine child', portraying the pure and trusting soul. The soul can then come into relationship with the suprasensible realm, shown in the sequence from the *Rosarium* as the divine child rising into a cloud. This depiction indicates that *Nigredo*, which involves the purification of base elements, has progressed into the second alchemical stage, *Albedo*, in which the soul awakens.

A sequence of three emblems illustrates the awakened soul, in the form of the Divine Child, ascending to receive the dew of Holy Spirit before re-entering the body. The return to the material world is symbolised by the two ravens at the sepulchre's base (Figures 18–20).

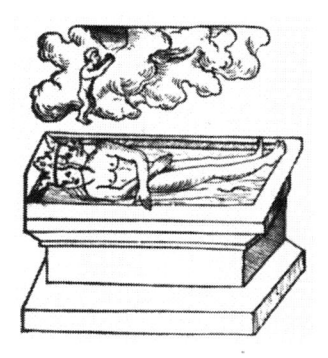

Figure 18. The Soul Ascends

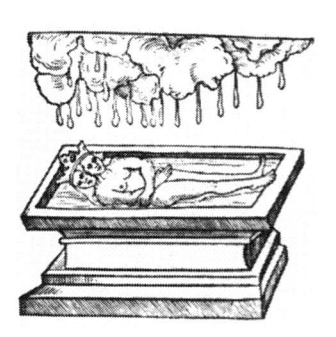

Figure 19. Divine Dew of *Albedo*

Figure 20. The Soul Returns

This alchemical sequence appears in the following lucid dream, but represented through my personal dream imagery:

With lucidity, my dream body disappears, and my soul is carried across the dazzling darkness at great speed. Finding my breath takes great focus. When I do so, the velvet blackness becomes deeply ecstatic. Suddenly, the lucid space opens into a vast hall, panelled in wood and with floor-to-ceiling windows. The hall has a large seating area with red cushions covering it. "What is it I'm meant to see?" I wonder.

To my surprise, a small infant appears before me on one of the cushions. Joy and love move through me as I recognise this child is both mine and not mine — he is the Christ child, so he belongs to everyone. He seems like an earthly child, in that he is completely pure and innocent, except that he is fully cognizant and aware of all life's mysteries and contradictions.

His blue eyes are radiant with love and intelligence. When I move to pick him up, he surprises me by standing up erect. We look at one another for a long time. Then he says in a clear voice, 'The blue is for ideas.' I am very curious about what the child means, and I would like to say in return, 'The blue is also Spirit', but I feel so startled by what he has said that my focus shifts, and I realise, sadly, that I'll soon be waking up. We continue to gaze at each other communicating in silence until the dream ends.

When I awaken, I am conscious that I have been in the refreshing presence of the 'Divine child'.

The end of the *Albedo* sequence in the *Rosarium* is personified by the image of a resurrected, winged hermaphrodite, next to which stands a moon-bearing fruit tree (Figure 21), alluding to the sacred teaching of Jesus, 'By their fruits you shall know them.'[119]

Figure 21. The Resurrected Hermaphrodite and the Moon Tree

The alchemical stage of *Citrinitas* that follows *Albedo* is depicted in the *Rosarium* by another sequence of emblems in which the cycle of purification, union and return occurs yet again. We now see the royal couple in sexual union, but this time with wings, floating on the water and able to move between land, water and air with ease (Figure 22).

Figure 22. The Winged Royal Couple

The second image from the second cycle shows a sepulchre on which the winged sun shines, emblematic of the all-encompassing illumination of Spirit in *Citrinitas* (Figure 23).

Figure 23. The Winged Sun

The next image replaces the sun with the winged hermaphrodite, again shown 'dead' on the sepulchre, but this time infused with Spirit (Figure 24).

Figure 24. The Winged Hermaphrodite on the Sepulchre

Then, once more, in the following emblem, the hermaphrodite lies wingless on the sepulchre; however this time, a mature female form, that of Sophia, symbolising the maturity and wisdom of the Soul, ascends into the cloud, returning with the gifts of the Spirit (Figures 25-27).

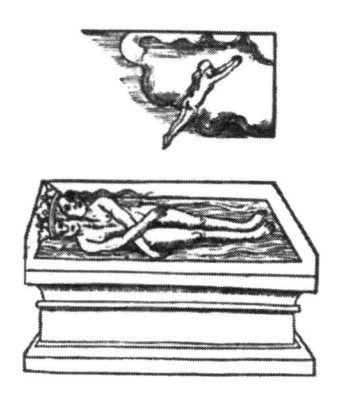

Figure 25. Wisdom Ascends

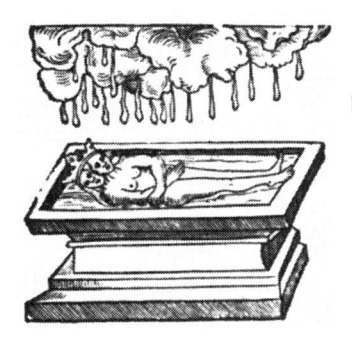

Figure 26. Divine Dew of *Citrinitas*

Figure 27. Wisdom Returns

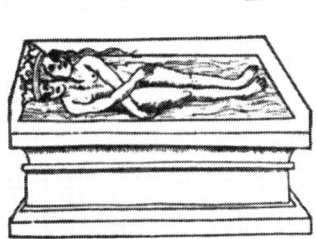

This marks the culmination of the *coniunctio* in which Soul and Spirit combine in the *unio mystica* or *mystical union* of oneness, which characterises *Citrinitas*. Words from St Teresa of Avila's treatise, *The Interior Castle*, describe this state:

> It is all a union of love with love, and its operations are entirely pure, and so delicate and gentle that there is no way of describing them; but the Lord can make the soul very deeply conscious of them.[120]

The following excerpt from a Lucid Surrender dream which I had some years into lucid dreaming called 'The Fingerprint of God' depicts an experience of *Citrinitas*:

In my dream, I'm unhappy to find myself in a shopping mall. I say, 'I know I'm dreaming, Lord, if you want to come for me.' To my amazement, my soul is lifted onto the winds of the Black Light as the dreamscape and my dream body falls away. The winds carry me very fast for a great distance and then descend steeply. I repeat a sacred song to keep my focus.

I am carried through an expanse of golden hexagons that remind me of a honeycomb. Eventually my soul is released again onto the Black Light, where I see a vast golden sphere with swirls of golden light in a pattern akin to the whorls of a fingerprint. The thought comes: 'The fingerprint of God!'

A ruby red light appears in its centre, and filling the spiral, it spills over its edges, embraces me, and pierces my heart. Part of me realises, 'This is what is meant by being in the sacred heart of Jesus!' There is tremendous humility, healing and hope in this realisation. Then I am moved back through the red light back into the shopping mall!

In *Citrinitas*, cosmic light forms appear in an infinite variety, according to the personality of the dreamer and the intent of the dream. Such light becomes one with the dreamer, dispelling the illusion of separateness, expanding the dreamer's understanding and energising the dreamer with Spirit — the true inner gold of alchemy. As the *Rosarium* emblems suggest, to engage with *Citrinitas* light forms requires ever-deepening surrender on the part of the dreamer, characterised by openness, curiosity, humility, devotion and gratitude.

At the end of the *Citrinitas* cycle displayed in the *Rosarium*, the resurrected hermaphrodite stands clothed in magnificent garments of the alchemical colours gold, red, white and black. The royal garments mirror an inner state of splendour, a merging of Soul and Spirit (Figure 28).

Figure 28. The Resurrected Hermaphrodite and the Sun Tree

To the left of the hermaphrodite, there stands a tree bearing many suns, suggestive of spiritual fruit brought into life. To the right, a pelican draws blood from its own breast to feed its young, a tale of one who gives their life over to a larger life purpose. This emblem marks the completion of the work. The Hermaphrodite is now awakened, ready to move into the stage of *Rubedo*, returning to the world in order to incarnate spiritual qualities in the physical world.

The *Rosarium* concludes with the transformative action of *Rubedo* by presenting the risen Christ stepping out of the sepulchre (Figure 29). He wears a red cloak signifying the world of manifestation, and bears the staff of divine guidance and the illumination of the Greater Wisdom. Jung describes 'the psychological position of the Christ symbol' as exemplifying 'the archetype of the self.' [121] In the *Rosarium*, the risen Christ is viewed as the Philosopher's Stone, whose power bestows not only eternal life but also love.

Figure 29. The Risen Christ

Similarly, on awakening from Lucid Surrender, we bring spiritual insights, the fruits of the moon and sun tree, into waking life much as the light of the sun and the cycles of the moon bring light and life to our world.

I recall a dream that fuelled much change in my own life. At the time, I was running a charitable counselling centre in London, and we were ten thousand pounds short of a fundraising target of fifty thousand pounds. I went to bed feeling despondent and weighed down by the responsibility, so I asked for guidance.

That night, I had a lucid dream in which a whirlwind formed on the Black Light, picking up many small notes of money as it twisted in space. I realised within the dream that we could raise the money quickly by making an appeal to the charity's many supporters to raise £10,000 in ten days, which, with the help of generous donors, we managed to do. The dream had inspired and energised the fundraising, bringing Spirit to life as the numerous donors gave out of their love for the charity's work.

Jung stated, 'What was divided on a lower level will reappear, united, on a higher one.' [122] Much as the alchemical 'royal marriage' brings the *Magnum Opus*, the Great Work of alchemy, to consummation through the union of opposites, [123] so in Lucid Surrender, Soul and Spirit come together united in love both in dreams and life.

NOTES:

106. A shorter version of this chapter was first given as a presentation at the 2012 International Association of Dreams annual conference in Berkeley, California. I later presented on this topic at the IASD's Psiber Dreaming Conference in the autumn of 2012. I have also written more on a Jungian view of dream lucidity in Mary M. Ziemer [Melinda Powell], 'Lucid Surrender and Jung's Alchemical *Coniunctio*' in *Lucid Dreaming: New Perspectives on Consciousness in Sleep*, Vol. 1, eds. Ryan Hurd and Kelly Bulkeley (Santa Barbara, CA: Praeger, 2014), 145-166
107. Paracelsus, *Selected Writings*, Bollingen Series XXVIII, ed. Jolande Jacobi, trans. Norbert Guterman (Princeton, NJ: Princeton University Press, 1988), 145-146.
108. This expression was first coined by John Keats and elaborated upon in his letter to his brother and sister, George and Georgina Keats, composed between 14 February and 3 May 1819, where Keats says, 'Call the world if you will Please "The Vale of Soul-making". Then you will find out the use of the world...' See *The Letters of John Keats*, ed. Robert Gittings (Oxford: Oxford University Press, 1970, 1982), 249-250. James Hillman featured the notion of 'Soul making' in his Archetypal Psychology.
109. For an enchanting treatise on the connection between alchemy and perfumery, refer to Maggie Aftel, *The Essence of Alchemy: A Book of Perfume* (New York, NY: North Point Press, 1991).
110. Jung, *The Collected Works*, Vol. 16, para. 399.
111. This process is outlined in detail in Edward Edinger's beautiful explication of Jung's *Mysterium Coniunctionis*, *The Mystery of the Coniunctio: Alchemical Image of Individuation* (Toronto, Canada: Inner City Books, 1994).
112. First published as *De Alchimia Opuscula complura veterum philosophorum* [...] *Rosarium Philosophorum Secunda Pars* or *A Collection of Rare Alchemical Tracts from Philosophers of Antiquity* [...] *The Rosary of the Philosophers, Part II* (Frankfurt: Cyriac Jacob, 1550). For an English translation of the work see *The Rosary of the Philosophers*, ed. Adam McClean from the 18th century Glasgow Ferguson MS (Edinburgh: Magnum Opus Sourceworks, 1980). The text is comprised of sage quotes and teachings from various alchemists — a Rosary or 'Rose Garden' of verses.
113. Jung, *The Collected Works*, Vol. 16, paras. 353-564.
114. Ibid, para. 355.
115. Edward F. Edinger, *The Mystery of the Coniunctio: Alchemical Image of Individuation* (Toronto: Inner City Books, 1994), 80.
116. Jung, *The Collected Works*, Vol. 16, para. 410.

117. James Hillman, *Re-Visioning Psychology* (NewYork: NY: HarperCollins, 1975), xvii. Hillman borrows this notion from the poet's John Keats. See end note No. 104.
118. See *C. G. Jung: The Seminars, Nietzsche's Zarathustra: Notes on the Seminar Given in 1934–39 by C. G. Jung*, Vol. 2, Part I (13 March 1935), ed. James L. Jarrett (New York, New York: Routledge, 1989), 443.
119. Matthew 7:16, New Heart English Bible.
120. See Avila's *Interior Castle: The Classic Text with Spiritual Commentary*, C.Ss.R (Notre Dame, Indiana: Ave Marie Press, Inc,. 2007), 153.
121. Carl Jung, *Aion*, 2nd ed. (Princeton: Princeton University Press, 1969), 36–37.
122. Jung, *The Collected Works*, Vol. 13, para. 238.
123. Jung, *The Collected Works*, Vol. 16, para. 398.

THROUGH THE MIRROR

Part III

THE MIRROR OF THE HEART

The image is the mirror,
though what is seen is neither the mirror
nor the one who is looking into the mirror.
Ponder on that and try to understand,
because that is the essence of the realm of secrets. [124]

— Hadrat Abd al-Qadir al-Jilani (12th-century Sufi mystic)

Chapter 9

THE SPIRITUAL SCIENCE OF MIRRORS [125]

The science of the Imagination is also the science of mirrors, of all mirroring "surfaces" and of the forms that appear in them. [126]
— Henry Corbin

Through the ages, spiritual traditions have referred to the enigmatic property of mirrors as a metaphor to convey spiritual truths. As the Taoist philosopher Chuang Tsu observed, 'The mind of a perfect man is like a mirror: It grasps nothing; it expects nothing. It reflects but does not hold.' [127] His words evoke the empty stillness of a mirror to describe clarity of mind.

According to monotheistic faiths, the human being, made in the image of God, has the potential to mirror divine qualities. In Judaism, the *Kabbalah* teaches that the natural world acts as a 'cosmic mirror', [128] which reveals and conceals the nature of the Divine. It is no wonder that in early Christian literature, *The Book of Wisdom*, Wisdom is extolled as follows:

> She is the reflection of the eternal light.
> A spotless mirror of the working of God.
> Image of goodness. [129]

The Sufi tradition speaks mysteriously of 'the mirror of nothingness' upon which God self-discloses.[130] The Sufi scholar Sayyed Hossein Nasr elaborates:

> Now a mirror is a surface that reflects what is placed before it, and in itself the surface is 'nothing,' that is, it has no form of its own. Since there cannot be any being independent of God, what we see as the cosmos therefore cannot but be but a reflection of God's Names and Qualities upon what is ontologically 'nothing,' like a mirror.[131]

For Sufis, not only creation, but also our dreams, act as mirrors that reflect qualities of the Divine.[132]

In this chapter, I invite you to explore with me the properties of light and symmetry in mirrors and how these appear in dreams and dreamwork.

Light and Mirrors

To begin, it is helpful to recall a simple fact: to produce a reflection in a mirror requires light. Without light, the mirror's surface appears dark. Fundamentally, what we see in a mirror is light. Physicists now know that most of the photons that strike the mirror's surface interact with electrons inside the glass and its silvered lining, and literally 'bend back' to the viewer (as in the Latin *reflectare*).[133] These actions combine to create the image reflected in a mirror. From the spiritual perspective, dreams both interpenetrate with, and reflect, the light of the Divine in 'the mirror of the heart'.[134]

This helps us understand the way dreams can function on a spiritual level by mirroring the inner light of the Spirit, as in this dream:

My eldest brother and I drive in a black, shiny Range Rover in the Alps at about 12,000 feet and going up. The icy road curves along the mountainside at twilight and the Alpen glow bathes the mountains in russet gold. The red-gold light shines so intensely along the top of the mountain peaks that it holds my gaze. I recognise radiance as a sign of the Spirit, becoming more lucid as I do so.

In another dream, hundreds of heart-shaped crystals hanging in a shop window caught and reflected a brilliant light, the beauty and intensity of which I realised to be nothing less than Spirit. Given such experiences, it makes perfect sense to me that the word *lucid* derives from the Latin root *luces*, meaning light.

The cleaner the mirror's surface, the clearer the reflection. Again speaking metaphorically, the 12th-century Sufi mystic and teacher Abd al-Qadir tells us: 'The man of knowledge makes images while the wise man polishes the mirror upon which the truth is reflected.'[135] We can 'polish' our inner mirror through spiritual practices of body and mind, including yoga, meditation and prayer.

In contrast, a tarnished or dirty surface 'blocks' or 'veils' the light, dimming the mirror. Another Sufi mystic, Ibn al-'Arabi, born in the 12th century, observes that 'an unpolished mirror' is like 'undifferentiated creation without anything of the

Spirit in it'. [136] This effect has occurred in my own dreams when, for example, I have recognised within the dream that the clutter filling a room symbolises my own cluttered thoughts. Realising this, I am able to become lucid and the dreamscape gives way to light.

Similarly, at other times, the winds on the Black Light may lose their power until I clear the way by invoking the pure light of the Spirit:

> *With lucidity, I bow my head and the dreamscape and my dream body give way to the Black Light. This time, though, the movement on the winds feels ponderous, like getting a heavy rocket to lift off. I realise I am not focused and so pray for the Spirit to 'lift me up'. In response, the energy carries my consciousness as if I were lying on a flying carpet into a very deep space. Just staying with this movement takes a good deal of energy. It feels as if my soul travels at the speed of light or even faster!*

Like a tarnished mirror, when the mind is overwrought and crowded with unhelpful thoughts, dreams tend to be less luminous. Yet, as in this dream, when we give our attention to the sacred, the dream becomes clearer. Abd al-Qadir explains further: 'When the mirror of the heart is completely cleansed by being polished with the continuous evocation of the divine Names, one has access to and knowledge of the divine attributes. The witnessing of this vision is only possible in the mirror of the heart.' [137] Fortunately, no matter how much polishing may be needed, provided that we try the best we can, grace may come to our aid and reveal the Spiritual realm.

Mirroring Symmetries

A basic principle of Nature, that of *symmetry*, becomes apparent in the property of 'mirror symmetry'. The word *symmetry* is made up of the prefix *sym*, meaning 'the same', and the root *metre* or *measure*. Every time we look at ourselves in a mirror, we see one of the most common forms of symmetry, known as 'bilateral symmetry' — a left/right reversal through 180 degrees.[138] This reversal is all the more extraordinary since it only applies to the horizontal plane — or else we would find ourselves reflected in a mirror upside down!

Many life forms display symmetry, conferring qualities of beauty, harmony, balance and wholeness — qualities of the Divine. Physicist and dream researcher Nigel Hamilton has identified symmetrical development as part of a natural and organic process whereby, through the evolution of symmetrical forms in our dreams, '*something is actually being constructed* in the psyche',[139] a growth in the personality mirrored in the geometry of the imagery that appears. The geometric forms in the dream that follows communicate and affirm my spiritual nature:

In my dream, someone hands me a letter in a blue envelope. I think of how a letter in a dream can bring guidance and so become lucid.

As I bow my head, the dreamscape falls away and in a flash the dreamscape and my dream body dissolve. Taken on winds through the Holy darkness, my soul is surrounded by a multi-faceted geometric structure radiating white beams of light on all sides. I hear myself singing, 'Holy, Holy, Holy, Lord God of Power and Might, Heaven and Earth are full of your glory.

Blessed is he who comes in the name of the Lord.'

Then the light form coalesces into a large sphere of purple silhouetted against a backdrop of velvety black. A red halo rings the purple. The purple elicits in me an awareness of suffering, and of the Divine. For some time, I meditate on the qualities of the colour.

The purple sphere changes into vivid joyful yellow, ringed with red. All the while, I am aware of light pulsating through my being. Although I long to stay in the experience, the yellow and red dissolve all around me and I awaken.

Of note, both the initial geometric form and the sphere it becomes are symmetrical structures. Later, I identified the former as a dodecahedron, one of the five Platonic solids. The 15th-century philosopher Marsilio Ficino viewed the dodecahedron as a mirror of the image of God because its shape most nearly approached a sphere [140] (the sphere being considered the most 'perfect' of forms because of its flawless internal symmetry).

In this dream, the dodecahedron and sphere give expression to a divine, harmonic order. Whenever I bring to mind the purple sphere that formed out of the dodecahedron, I feel calmed and strengthened, my mind clear, my heart renewed, ready for whatever life may bring.

Mirroring and Healing

The property of mirroring is a helpful analogy for working therapeutically with dreams. Such dreamwork can dramatically change the dreamer's sense of who they are by helping them to see themselves in a new way. This finds a parallel in infant psychology, described by the psychoanalyst D. W. Winnicott, who observed, 'In individual emotional development *the precursor of the mirror is the mother's face.*' [141]

Winnicott showed that the infant's self-perception depends on a process of reciprocal mirroring between mother (or caregiver) and baby, through facial expressions, voice tone, holding, handling and gestures, all of which leads to the child growing in self-esteem while developing the capacity for intimacy, creative reciprocity, and trust in relationships. More than simply 'seeing' one another, the baby and mother see 'into' each other emotionally, and so apprehend each other more fully.

Similarly, dreams can provide us with positive mirroring that a therapist then encourages. For example, one woman I was working with dreamed that her ex-partner embraced her from behind. Turning around, she was surprised to see he was wearing her glasses. In this example, both the dream, as a mirror of the dreamer's personal psychology, and our therapeutic reflections on it provided 'mirroring' that enabled her to gain new insight into the qualities in herself of which she had previously been unaware. This woman, who longed to be seen and known, came to understand that the qualities she so admired in her partner were the very qualities she herself possessed.

When children haven't received enough healthy mirroring, as adults it can be hard for them to feel seen or even to see themselves. This was the case for one of my clients, a gifted artist, who had a hard time 'seeing' this gift in herself. She had no memory of her parents ever sitting down with her to help her do colouring or admire her artwork. In therapy it was important for her to discover her art through my eyes, by having me watch her draw and show my appreciation for her talent. Through my more positive mirroring of the 'mother-image',[142] she learned to recognise her gift, express her creativity more fully and to see herself in a new light, a capacity that also came to be apperceived through her dreams.

An image viewed in a mirror may also powerfully capture the essence of a psychological complex, of a distorted self-perception, as in this dream that I had in my mid-twenties, not long after I had joined the United States Peace Corps in Poland:

It is a dark night, and I am in a house like the one where I grew up, but this one is full of maze-like passages. Confused, I walk through the house holding a lantern. Unexpectedly, I come upon a large mirror in which I am startled to see my reflection. I wear a long, white, Victorian-style nightgown. My figure is superimposed over the faces of my parents, who look upset. The mirror's background is completely black apart from the glow of the candle. In my left hand, I hold a glass of water in which a streak of blood has begun to spread. I am horrified to realise that I must drink this water and wake up.

Puzzling over this dream, I saw the mirror's darkness as reflecting the weight of the painful family conflicts that I had carried with me, despite my new life in Poland.

I now see the dream as a sign that I needed to be more in touch with my physicality and femininity, my instinctual nature, and I understand that my strong revulsion mirrored my inability to embody this. Working with this dream in therapy many years later, I was able to re-engage with it as a portal to free myself from my unconscious inhibitions and to truly inhabit my body.

Other mirroring dreams can hold both personal and transpersonal meanings, reflecting our divinity, as in this lucid dream of mine:

> *With lucidity, my soul is taken into a shimmering field of ecstatic Black Light, where I lose all sense of myself as a being in space and time. Two large transparent cubes appear, floating and rotating slowly against the black. As I look more closely, I see that the sides of each cube are reflecting back to me three-dimensional scenes from my life.*
>
> *As I watch, commonplace scenes, such as my walking along a busy London road with its traffic, trash and worn-out crowds, take on the most beautiful cast, as though even the coarsest reality is capable of radiating breath-taking splendour. I am filled with profound joy. Everything makes perfect sense and I realise it all means the same, single thing: love. I have a profound desire to bring what I've just learned into life by sharing this awareness.*

In this dream, the details of my personal life were being viewed through the lens of a 'Higher Awareness'. As my memories replayed, infused with the compassionate perspective of Spirit, I was put in touch with the loving consciousness that rests at the core of existence, leaving me impelled to share this sense of life's preciousness.

Re-Framing Our Capacities

From a psychotherapeutic perspective, the frame of a mirror represents our capacity to contain what is being reflected to us by the mirror, whether pertaining to our personal psychology or our spiritual potential. For each person, depending on their personality and situation in life, the form and structure of the mirror holds a specific meaning. For instance, a mirror without a frame may signify a fragile sense of self on the one hand, or an openness towards the transpersonal on the other. Symmetrical mirrors and frames can both foster and reveal a movement towards inner balance and harmony. The material of the frame, whether of wood, glass, or metal will also have personal resonances.

The colour of a mirror's frame can be linked with alchemical symbolism as outlined in Part II. For example, a dull, darkened frame foreshadows the 'captive light' of *Nigredo*, whereas one of shiny black, like obsidian, can presage Divine darkness. A silver frame may prefigure qualities associated with the stage of *Albedo* and the opening of the soul. A golden frame may herald a powerful experience of the Divine as encountered in *Citrinitas*. Only an exploration of the *dreamer's associations* with the mirror's frame can reveal the full range of psycho-spiritual undertones.

Dreams of a specific time in the dreamer's past may indicate that feelings from that time have a special bearing on the present. Over the years, I have dreamed a number of times about a mirror that I bought in my teens. (I had always longed for an Edwardian-style mahogany mirror set on a large antique dresser and a four-poster bed.) By working at summer jobs, I saved up enough money to buy a beautiful three-part mirror, four feet in height and six in width. The mirror's frame was curved along the top, with straight vertical sides. Two smaller side mirrors flanked the large central mirror. The dresser and mirror stood opposite a four-poster bed I had also managed to buy.

Although I didn't realise it at the time, I can now see that the bedroom furniture stood for the vision of the ideal marriage I so desired. With hindsight, I can also see that the symmetrical proportions of the Edwardian design appealed to my longing for balance, harmony and beauty. Dreaming of this mirror over time has reminded me to hold on to my ideals even as they helped to develop the maturity and wisdom I would need to realise this vision at long last in my life.

The next two chapters that follow apply the properties of light and symmetry to a series of dreams, each featuring a mirror, beginning with an in-depth analysis of the dream that initiated this cycle, the one in which the Edwardian-style mirror figures so prominently. By peering into these dream-mirrors, we shall see how they both reflect the trajectory of our personal psychology and can become thresholds to new dimensions of Being, open to us all through the 'mirror of the heart'.

Notes:

124. Al-Qadir, *The Secret*, 54.
125. This chapter is a compilation of the workshop 'Though a Glass Lucidly' that I gave at the 2013 International Association of Dreams Psiber Dreaming Conference and an article by the same name in *Lucid Dreaming Experience*, 2, No. 2 (September 2013): 9–15.

126. A quote from Corbin's masterly *Alone with the Alone: Creative Imagination in the Sufism of Ibn Arabi*, trans. Willard Trask (Princeton: Princeton University Press, 1969), 218.
127. From *Chuang Tsu Inner Chapters: A Companion Volume to the Tao Te Ching*, trans. Gia-Fu Feng and Jane English (San Francisco, California: Amber Lotus Publishing, 2000), 159.
128. Daniel Chanad Matt cites this Taoist teaching in his study of the Kabbalistic commentary, *The Book of Mirrors: Sefer 'Mar ot ha-Zove' ot*, by R. David ben Yehuda he Hasid (Chico, California: Scholar Press, 1982), 9.
129. Chapter 7:26, Revised Standard Version
130. Sayyed Hossein Nasr, *The Garden of Truth: The Vision and Promise of Sufism, Islam's Mystical Tradition* (New York, NY: Harper One, 2007), 43.
131. Ibid., 43
132. William C. Chittick in his *Imaginal Worlds: Ibn al-'Arabi and the Problem of Religious Diversity* (Albany, New York: Suny Press, 1994), 25.
133. See Richard P. Feynman's, *The Strange Theory of Light and Matter* (Great Britain: Penguin Books, 1990), 16 & 76.
134. Al-Qadir, *The Secret*, 76.
135. Ibid., 76.
136. From Arabi's *The Bezels of Wisdom* (Classics of Western Spirituality), trans. R. W. J. Austin (Mahwah, New Jersey: Paulist Press, Inc., 1980), 50.
137. Al-Qadir, *The Secret*, 76.
138. Richard L. Gregory, 'Shaving in a Mirror with Ockham's Razor', in Miranda Anderson (ed.), *An Interdisciplinary Collection Exploring the Cultural Story of the Mirror* (Newcastle: Cambridge Scholars Publishing, 2008), 94–104.
139. Nigel Hamilton, 'Psychospiritual Transformation: Light, Colour, and Symmetry', in Robert J. Hoss and Robert P. Gongloff (eds), *Dreams: Understanding Biology, Psychology, and Culture*, Vol. 2 (Santa Barbara, CA: ABC-CLIO, LLC, 2019), 634–640. Italics in original.
140. Jacomien Prins, 'Mirrors as Transmitters of Divine Harmony' in Miranda Anderson, *An Interdisciplinary Collection Exploring the Cultural Story of the Mirror* (Newcastle: Cambridge Scholars Publishing, 2008), 80–91.
141. From Winnicott's 'Mirror-role of Mother and Family in Child Development', in *Playing and Reality* (London and New York: Routledge Classics edition, 1971, 2005), 149–159.
142. Ibid., 153. As Winnicott claims, '...when the average girl studies her face in the mirror she is reassuring herself that the mother-image is there and that the mother can see her and that the mother is *en rapport* with her.'

Chapter 10

THE MIRROR AND THE SNAKE: PERSONAL REFLECTIONS ON A WAKING DREAM

*The face, therefore, is the image of the heart,
and the eyes are the mirror of the soul and its affections.*[143]

— Fr. Cornelius a Lapide, S.J.

Sometimes, a dream may open our hearts, helping us to see ourselves anew and changing the direction of our lives. One such dream came to me on Good Friday, 2006. At the time of the dream, I was twelve years into my first marriage and had recently started my training in transpersonal psychotherapy.

The dream, which I have entitled 'The Mirror and the Snake', features the Edwardian-style mirror described in the preceding chapter:

In the dream, I 'wake up' in the early hours of the morning to find myself in the bed of the 'ideal' bedroom I had created for myself as a teenager. The white shutters are drawn to the sides of the window, open to the moonlight. The air feels soft and fluid like water, the atmosphere peaceful. I am lying on the antique, four-poster bed that I bought in my teens. My (then) husband sleeps on my right.

The beauty of the silvery moonlight reflected in the large mirror on my dresser opposite the bed catches my eye. The mirror has a strong wooden frame curved along the top with straight sides, flanked by a smaller side mirror along each side, like a triptych over an altar. My reverie comes to an abrupt halt when I see a large rattlesnake coiled up on the dresser at the foot of the mirror.

The snake has been waiting for me, and when I look at it, lifts its head slightly. I freeze with fear. Mesmerised, I watch as the snake, glowing white in the moonlight, slides down the dresser onto the floor gracefully and purposefully.

I pray that if I stay very still, it will leave the room, but it slithers along the left side of my bed towards me. I desperately want my husband to wake up, but he doesn't stir. As I watch rigid with fear, the snake climbs up my nightstand and curls around the bedside lamp's base, before moving onto my bed, where it coils up again. Suddenly, it rears back to strike. I am terrified, convinced I will die as the snake lunges towards the space between my brows. Abruptly, I wake from my dream.

Afterwards, the dream haunted me. At the time, I viewed the snake as a harbinger of evil and the dream as a nightmare. It felt as though the snake's fangs had lodged in my brow between the eyes, and I could not get them out. I rubbed that space often, wondering what would have happened if I hadn't woken up in fear.

I took the dream to the psychotherapist I was seeing and

although we considered the dream from many angles, and drew many insights from it, the dream still felt incomplete and frightening to me.

The dream so troubled me that I overcame my shyness and volunteered to take part in a Waking Dream Process at a training workshop given at CCPE, under the guidance of the centre's director, Nigel Hamilton.[144]

Apart from what I had learned from an introductory lecture about this particular dream re-entry technique, I did not have much idea of what to expect. I knew that Hamilton, who had pioneered the Waking Dream Process, would be supporting me as my dream guide, helping me contain the feelings brought up by the dream and to track them in my body. However, I had no idea how this would work in practice.

The Waking Dream Experience from the 'Inside Out'

At the outset, I was terrified to face the snake again, but my need for the dream to be resolved and my curiosity overcame my fear.[145] Hamilton suggested I sit down opposite him and invited me to retell the dream. He asked me what was going on in my life around the time of the dream, and I explained that I had been having difficulties in my marriage.

As my guide, he then asked me to close my eyes and to describe the dream again in more detail, focusing on the setting and atmosphere. I started by recalling how the dream began, with my 'waking up' as I lay in bed, aware of the still moonlight filling the room. When I described the beauty of the moonlight reflected in the mirror at the foot of my bed, he asked me to locate that feeling in my body. I gestured to my solar plexus and was instructed to keep my right hand there throughout the visualisation to anchor this feeling. Doing so helped to calm me, and although I became very tense and fearful at times during the exploration of the dream, my hand resting on my belly provided me with reassurance.

When asked for more details about the bedroom, I shared the story of the room, adding wryly that it represented my 'fantasy' of what I had hoped marriage could be like. Hamilton reminded me that no matter what difficulties I might be going through, I should hold on to my ideals.

Next, we moved on to the moment that the snake lifted its head to look at me. When I visualised this, I lurched back in my chair. I was asked to 'freeze-frame' what I had seen, and to describe what I was now experiencing in my body.

As I re-imagined my eyes meeting the snake's, an immense rush of powerful energy filled my chest, my throat, and the back of my head, pushing me backwards. This rush of energy frightened me even more than the snake! I started shaking, feeling sweaty and cold at the same time, as though my body was being split in two.

Hamilton explained that I did not need to be afraid, since the snake was a part of me and wouldn't hurt me. That comforted me. He asked if I could be open to the experience, adding that I did not have to fight the snake, but that I simply needed to relax. After some time, my breathing calmed, and I felt at ease.

I 'watched' the snake begin to uncoil and slide down the dresser to the floor. As it approached me, the pressure in my head, throat and chest intensified. Hamilton encouraged me to breathe deeply and slowly, in through my nose and out through my mouth, reminding me that I did not need to be afraid and that things would go much easier if I accepted what was happening and could allow the snake to do what it needed.

Turning back towards the snake, I saw that it had climbed up on the nightstand, where it coiled up around the base of the lamp. Sensing my tension, Hamilton said again that the snake was a part of me and so would not harm me. He reminded me to breathe!

The snake moved onto the bed, where it coiled up again, calmly eyeing me. I waited but the snake did not move. In a flash, it reared back and leapt up towards me. This time it slipped in, between my brows, curled up in my head and dropped its tail down the length of my spine. A fountain of light and energy surged up along the snake and through my body.

The sensation lasted for some minutes but felt timeless. When it ended, I became aware that I was back in the room. I found myself saying, 'The snake didn't destroy me.' My guide simply replied, 'Of course not, it's part of you.'

I felt quietly content and at ease. Coming out of the visualisation, I had the sense of being a different person, or rather more fully me. Hamilton remarked that the dream suggested a significant change would happen in my life, that I had been awakened on a soul level and needed to be aware of that.

This was a new idea for me, and one that I could now understand on an energetic level. For the first time since childhood, it felt that my soul had fully entered my physical body. I was amazed by how intensely real the visualisation had been — so different from simply working associatively with the dream. The process had left me powerfully embodied, my mind clear.

In the question-and-answer period that followed, a member of the audience wanted to know if this had been an experience of *Kundalini*. Hamilton explained that *Kundalini* was rooted in yogic teachings on the 'energetic body', and that when this energy, depicted as a coiled snake sleeping at the base of the spine, was 'awakened' and unleashed, it had the power to bring union (yoga) with the Divine.

Previously, I considered such teachings to belong to the 'occult' and had treated them with scepticism. What mattered now was that far from viewing the snake as evil, I had encountered an emissary of the Spirit, bringing a new sense of wholeness and awakening me to new possibilities. A dream that I had perceived as a nightmare had turned out to hold great healing potential, once I had overcome my fearful projections. With my guide's help, I was able to meet the snake on its own terms as both earthly and spiritual, and as part of myself.

This dream initiated a period of great growth and change in my life, one that continues to this day. Through the learning of the many lucid dreams that that were to follow, I developed the practice of Lucid Surrender. In my professional work, an outpouring of creativity enabled me to run a charitable counselling centre and later to co-found the Dream Research Institute with Nigel Hamilton at CCPE.

Seven years after the dream, I divorced and, in time,

married again, finding personal fulfilment I had not known before. Over time, I became an author, writing about dreams and dream lucidity. This seminal dream continues to inspire me to look beyond my fears, and to 'wake up' to the beauty and power of the Spirit mirrored in the dream. I hope that it may encourage you to discern the presence of Soul as you reflect on your own dreams and the longings of your heart.

NOTES:

143. *Commentaria in Scripturam Sacram*, Paris 1878, vol. 9, 541. As it appears in Tradition in Action: https://www.traditioninaction.org/religious/n002rpLapide_Appearance.htm
144. See Nigel Hamilton's, *Awakening Through Dreams: The Journey Through the Inner Landscape* (London: Karnac Books, 2014).
145. The audio of this session can be found on the DRI website: www.driccpe.org.uk

Chapter 11

Through the Looking Glass in Lucidity[146]

For now we see through a glass, darkly; but then face to face: now I know in part; but then shall I know even as also I am known.
— 1 Corinthians 13:12, King James Version

Legends of magical mirrors as portals to new worlds come to life in stories like Lewis Carroll's *Alice Through the Looking Glass*, but what happens when, in lucidity, we pass as Alice did, through a mirror? In this chapter, I will share nine dreams that I had over a twenty-year period, each of which involves a mirror, whose reflection points to a deeper knowledge both of oneself and of the Divine.

The Other Side of the Glass

Encounters with mirroring properties in dreams such as the following made me curious about what lay 'behind' the 'surface' of the dream. Here is a dream from my early forties which holds great significance for me in this regard:

In the dream, I am an adult and stand in darkness looking at a closed window blind, wary of the bright light filtering through its seams and tears in the fabric. I recognise the blind as familiar to me from a very early memory, dating back to when I was still learning to walk.

Next, a white beam of fiery laser-white light from behind the blind cuts a vertical line along the far-left side of the blind, and I feel terribly frightened. Then another horizontal line forms at a right angle to the first and I realise that an uppercase 'H' is taking shape. An 'O' immediately follows, and then, in a flash, the word 'Holy Spirit' beams out at me.

The context of my recollection within this dream is important here. I remember my mother putting me down in my crib for my afternoon nap and lowering the window blind against the hot California sun. The light shining through the small rips in the blind and along its edges terrified me. In great fear, I would scramble out of the crib and crawl along the hall to find my mother. My mother, unaware of my fear (especially as I didn't cry), picked me up and put me back in the crib, only to have me crawl out again.

As a child, I was intensely afraid of the dark and frightened of mirrors. The mirror in *Snow White and the Seven Dwarfs* left me apprehensive, and the escapades of Alice in the looking glass world of Lewis Carroll deeply unsettled me. But the worst association with mirrors came when I was about ten years old and had gone to an all-girl sleepover. One of the girls whispered that if you chanted 'Bloody Mary' before a mirror in a dark room, the image of Bloody Mary would appear in the mirror. The girls dared one another to look in the mirror. I couldn't bring myself to do so. After that, I felt afraid to enter a dark room if it had a mirror in it.

At fifteen, I started feeling more comfortable with mirrors when, after saving money to buy new furniture, I redecorated my bedroom, choosing the large antique dresser with a matching mirror and the four-poster bed described in the previous chapter.

Reflecting on the dream of the window blind many years later, it struck me that for the words *Holy Spirit* to have appeared to me as they did in that dream, the letters must have been cut through from behind in the form of mirror writing. Importantly, I could now understand that what had begun in infancy as a nameless and incomprehensible fear had been transformed mirror-wise into a profound awareness of spiritual illumination.

Some years after this, I had a dream which further revealed the presence of an invisible reality beyond the looking glass:

In the dream, I exit the main sanctuary of the Baptist church where I grew up, entering the foyer. The window along the length of the entranceway has become a mirror, with floor-to-ceiling side mirrors.

An intense white light radiates from the mirror and nearly blinds me. The light feels like a purifying infusion of the Spirit. At the same time, I am aware that the light is not so much reflected from the mirror as radiating through it, which leaves me very curious about the world beyond the mirror.

Here, instead of a darkened blind, the three-part mirror stands as a threshold to the spiritual realm, whose light shines from 'beyond' the mirror. As the clarity and simplicity of this dream reflects, by this time, through many dreams and much therapeutic work, I was more able to work through my conditioned responses to dream imagery and, consequently, had become more open to the manifestation of Spirit.

Dreams as Mirrors of Psycho-Spiritual Development

Tracking my own mirror dreams over a twenty-year period, I can see that the earlier dreams harken back to my self-image, portraying scenes from childhood, or images of myself in my youth, in which I appear in loose-fitting gowns, rather disembodied and ugly to my own eyes. It was many years before I could see and recognise embodied reflections of my beauty, outwardly and inwardly, as shown by this dream:

> *I wear a white, close-fitting dress to a wedding where I will be speaking. (The dress looks like one that I bought in my twenties but that I only felt comfortable wearing in my forties.)*
>
> *The wedding takes place in a large church, similar to the one that I went to as a child. During the ceremony, I give a teaching on the Holy Spirit. Afterwards, a man walks up to me and says, 'You still have no idea of the impression you make on people. How full of the Spirit you are. How you touch people and how beautiful you are. How you change the room when you walk in.'*
>
> *In the next scene, I am standing in the church's bridal dressing room, thinking that I'd like a more colourful dress. I*

notice that I have bare feet and that my white dress is inside out! For a moment I am terribly embarrassed, but then I think, 'Well, the man still said what he said, even so.'

Although the wedding in my dream was not my own, from the alchemical perspective, all weddings in dreams herald the 'chymical wedding', in which the 'marriage' of two elements symbolises the union of the King and Queen in wedlock. In the alchemical stage of *Albedo*, the whitening, this marriage represents the union of body and soul. In the words of a 17th-century alchemist:

> This day, today
> Is the Royal Wedding day.
> For this thou wast born
> And chosen of God for joy [147]

A wedding in a dream also celebrates a deeper alignment between our inner nature and our outer life. As I understood it to be, the close-fitting dress, worn inside-out, was mirroring my efforts to reveal the soul's inner beauty to the outer world.

Not long after this dream, I started directing a charitable counselling centre for adults of all ages. It was a time of bringing many people together for a common purpose. The work was very hands-on, demanding and satisfying. The centre's capacity increased by 100 percent, funds were raised and links made with the local community. This activity is both reflected in and encouraged by the next mirror dream:

> *I enter a large hall where a band prepares for a celebration. Along the opposite side of the room, sliding glass doors open onto a sunlit garden. At either end of the hall, floor-to-ceiling mirrors line the walls. As I walk to the middle of the room, I can see that I am wearing blue worker's clothes.*
>
> *Seized by the urge to dance, I think how sad it is that people of all ages don't dance together as they did in the past. I decide that it's time to create a new dance! In spite of my heavy boots, I pirouette to the band's music like a ballerina. Spinning clockwise with my arms open wide, I realise I'm dreaming and, raising my hands above me with my palms pressed together, wait for the Spirit to seize my soul. But to my disappointment, I awaken!*

In this dream, the dance represents the 'dance of life'. The spiritual energy of this dream contributed to an outpouring of creative work in the community, supported by the many synchronicities and open-hearted support that helped the centre to thrive.

Even so, during this time and, indeed, throughout my life, I have found that being empowered by dreams is not always easy. The mirror dreams that followed this 'chymical wedding' indeed turned me 'inside out', challenging my ideas about reality and expanding my understanding of God to encompass the mystery of 'Divine Darkness'.

Passing Through the Mirror

The lucid dream described in this next section marks the first time that I experienced a mirror as a literal portal to a new dimension. Once again, the mirror featured in this dream was like the mirror I had in my bedroom as a teenager. I was in my early forties at the time of the dream and exhausted from managing the counselling centre. Not long after the dream, I came down with pneumonia. This dream gave me much comfort during my illness:

Resting on the four-poster bed in the bedroom from my late teens, I notice a vase of blue and yellow glass roses on my dresser and go over to look at them. The beauty of the antique-style mirror over the dresser, and the still light it reflects, catches my attention.

When I see my own reflection in the glass. I become lucid and bow my head in surrender, aware that mirrors can serve as portals to new dimensions. My Soul is pulled through the mirror and carried, as though on a magic carpet, across a field of Black Light. Brightly coloured, multi-dimensional geometric shapes fill the gleaming darkness. Passing through an immense dodecahedron, I find myself in a place much like the Baptist church I attended in childhood.

A handful of women, exuding strength and independence, come out to greet me as if they already know me, stroking my face, hands and arms. Their touch feels like the breath of the Holy Spirit, and I think of a line from a poem I once wrote: 'The Spirit puts on your hands like gloves.' A new line comes: 'Touch skin.'

As the women touch me, I sense they also receive something from me in a wordless, tactile exchange. We have all come to this place to learn of God. Teresa of Avila's poetry springs to mind:

'Teach me, God, all you know.' In that instance, I tumble out of the mirror, back into the original dream.

In the dream, captivated by the beauty of Spirit revealed in the mirror, I became lucid. Far from 'seeing into the mirror darkly',[148] I had been transported to a place of learning and healing.

Mirrors in Lucidity: Thresholds to Eternity

Through my lucid encounters involving mirrors, I have come to understand that how we interact with mirrors in our dreams affects what they reveal to us, as in this next dream:

I carry a young girl playfully on my back as we run back and forth across a large room of neo-classical design. White curtains billow in the floor-to-ceiling windows, and, along with our laughter, I can hear the sound of my footfall on the wooden floor. The room has no furniture, but as I run across the room with the child, I notice that a large oval mirror with a gilt frame hangs on the wall. Recognising the significance that a mirror holds, I set the child down and return to contemplate the mirror.

Once more, as I stand opposite a dream mirror, its beauty sparks lucidity. Although I realise that I can enter the mirror, I feel too weary to do so, and tell myself to 'wait on the Lord, for if the Lord wants me this way, the Lord will take me!' After a pause with my head bowed, my soul is lifted into the mirror and taken into a blackly lit space, alive with the gentle wind of the Spirit.

At first the refrain, 'Oh Holy One' comes to mind, but

then I remain silent, feeling ecstatic. Although the pleasure is exquisite, I understand that I am there not only to be uplifted by the ecstasy but also to bring this infusion of Spirit into waking reality through my work.

After some time, I am returned across the illumined darkness, where I see the mercury-like surface of the mirror's backing ahead of me! To my surprise, I tumble back through the mirror into the original dream.

This dream, as with the previous one, suggests that when we approach a mirror in a dream, we must first become still, like the mirror itself, before we can see beyond it. In stillness, the contemplation of Beauty opens us up to the presence of Spirit. The mirror itself marks a limen or threshold between the personal and the transpersonal, bringing the opportunity to see into ourselves as human and divine.

In the 12th century, a time when fine mirrors were rare and considered precious, the Sufi teacher Abd al-Qadir described human nature as a mirror that shows two sides — both what seems dense and coarse as well as that which seems fine and exquisite.[149] Such 'mirroring' in dreams may reflect not only the desires of the ego but also the soul's longing to be seen and known — to have its divinity revealed.

The longing to know our divine nature differs from the longing portrayed in J. K. Rowling's *Harry Potter and the Philosopher's Stone*, in which 'The Mirror of Erised' shows us the deepest and most desperate desire of our hearts.[150] In Potter's world, the mirror does not reveal knowledge or Truth — only desire. Those who gaze into the Mirror of Erised may end up driven mad 'not knowing if what it shows is real or even possible'.[151]

Very differently, when the heart's desire aligns with that of the Highest Will, then a mirror in a dream can move us beyond our limited perception. Here, I'll share a dream which begins with a mirror very like the Mirror of Erised, but which, through lucidity and my request for guidance, is transformed into a portal for Spirit:

> *I go to bed asking the Lord for guidance. In the dream, I find myself in a dance class, where a man approaches me from behind and wraps his arms lovingly around me. He turns me round to the right, towards a wall-sized mirror. I wonder if I'll be able to see who is holding me, but the man has tucked his head down behind my own. Although I do not know this man, I have a sudden yearning to make love to him. But looking deeply into the mirror, I become lucid and am pulled through the mirror, along with the man who continues to embrace me.*
>
> *Now invisible, the two of us travel on the Black Light, passing by spiralling sheaths of light. I recognise the touch of an angelic being whose forefinger takes my own in the blazing blackness. In reply, my finger signals, 'Where shall we go?' and the angel's finger communicates playfully, 'Where would you like?'*

In this dream, physical desire yields to a greater need — a longing for union with the Divine. For each of us, the desire to love, expressed in our longing and love for others, ultimately begins and ends in God's love.

Mirroring Infinity

Through my own lucid dreams, I have discovered that mirrors not only initiate lucidity but also serve as portals from within the lucid dream. I would like to report in full a lucid dream I have called, 'The Fingerprint of God', part of which I shared in Chapter Eight:

In my dream, I'm unhappy to find myself in a shopping mall. Then I become lucid and say, 'I know I'm dreaming, Lord, if you want to come for me.' My soul is seized onto the winds of the Black Light. The winds carry me very fast for a great distance and then descend steeply. I repeat a sacred song to keep my focus.

I am carried through an expanse of golden hexagons that remind me of a honeycomb. Eventually, I am whisked into an unadorned tabernacle, with dark wood walls, a floor of lapis lazuli edged with mother of pearl, and a vaulted ceiling of sky-blue and white. The winds bring me to the front of the sanctuary, where two celestial Beings open a small arched door.

With great joy I think, 'The Holy of Holies! I am being permitted to enter in!' I can see that behind the altar is a mirror, out of which shines an intense, white light. An Old Testament teaching comes to mind that says a searing light kills those who enter the tabernacle's inner sanctum unsanctified. For a moment, I feel afraid, aware of my impurity. However, my joy outweighs my concern. I trust that this is where I should be, since the dream has brought me here.

As I am brought closer to the mirror, I see my mother (who died some years before) smiling radiantly at me, a backdrop of azure blue framing her blonde hair. I realise that I am about to pass through the mirror's surface and join my mother, and because my mother is dead, I wonder, 'Does this mean I have died?'

My soul is taken through the mirror's white light and released into the Black Light. When I regain my equilibrium, an effulgent black cloud envelopes me in love. I know this cloud from other dreams as Divine presence. I repeat, 'Oh Holy One' and sing out hymns of praise with delight, with the cloud whirling around and through me in a kind of dance.

Suspended in the cloud, I am amazed to see a vast golden sphere with swirls of golden light in a pattern akin to the whorls of a fingerprint. The thought comes: 'The fingerprint of God! This is the true Holy of Holies.'

A ruby red ball of light appears in its centre and divides into two, emitting light that fills the spiral, spilling over its edges, embracing me, and piercing my heart. Part of me realises, 'This is what is meant by being in the sacred heart of Jesus!' There is profound humility, healing and hope in this realisation. With this I am moved swiftly back through the red into the shopping mall, and at this point, I know I have not died!

I have found that passing through a mirror in lucidity is to enter a sacred, inner sanctum, the wellspring of all Creation.

The Mirror and the Snake Revisited

Five years after the dream of 'The Mirror and the Snake' presented in the previous chapter, I had a lucid dream in which a mirror and snake feature, but in a new way:

In the dream, I am standing in a living room opposite a wall that is made of a floor-to-ceiling mirror. It takes me moment to realise that I am looking at a mirror, because I don't see my reflection, so it looks as though the room simply extends beyond the mirror.

But as I realise that it actually is a mirror that has doubled the size of the room, I become lucid. Spontaneously, I call out, 'Okay, God, let's go!' and my being is pulled through the mirror. On the 'other side', I am carried on the Black Light and winds, and a feeling of ecstasy overcomes me.

After a long transit, I find myself in a dream body lying in a foetal position on a floor covered with large square tiles. Each 'tile' is patterned with a mandala, having four parts radiating outwards from the centre in black, white, beige and brown. To my amazement, the tile that I am resting on begins to undulate, and, turning to the right, I see a snake with a head as large as my own looking at me. But, unlike in the dream of the rattlesnake so many years before, this time I feel perfectly safe. The snake sniffs gently around my face with its long, dark tongue, like a mother with her young. I sense the snake won't harm me as it embraces me in its coils.

Upon waking, I was reminded of the symbol of the ouroboros, the snake that swallows its own tail in an eternal round. I knew that a process deep in me had come full circle, and that I was now being shown, very tangibly, how Spirit carries us lovingly and protectively, nurturing us as we make our way through life.[152]

After so many lucid dreams, whenever I see a mirror in a

dream, I am now more able to say to myself, 'Wait a minute, there's something important here', taking time to contemplate what the mirror unveils. In waking life, too, mirrors now decorate my home, reminding me of the profound mystery of life and the 'world beyond'.

When we have learned to recognise the mirror as a herald of Spirit, we can trust that the mirror itself, ever calm and clear, unfailingly reveals, without judgement, the state of our hearts, helping each of us fully to know ourselves even as we are fully known.

Notes:

146. Originally published as 'Through a Glass Lucidly' in *Lucid Dreaming Experience*, 2, No. 2 (September 2013): 9–15.
147. *The Chymical Wedding of Christian Rosenkreutz*, originally published in German in 1616. This edition derives from an English translation published in 1690. This text is in the public domain. Acrobat edition prepared by Benjamin Rowe, October 2000. https://39514839f4a6dc8a84ae-eaa972a576b84b28f1b3596cd9812f8f.ssl.cf5.rackcdn.com/chymical_wedding.pdf
148. 1 Corinthians 13:12, King James Version.
149. Al-Qadir, *The Secret*, 62.
150. Rowling, J. K., *Harry Potter and the Philosopher's Stone* (London: Bloomsbury Publisher's, 1997), 156–157.
151. Ibid.
152. This dream amplified my understanding of an emblem found in Michael Maier's *Atalanta Fugiens: Sources of an Alchemical Book of Emblems* of a woman lying dead in an open grave with a serpent coiling around her (See Emblem L, Figure 50, 426). Rather than depicting a gruesome death scene, the emblem shows the woman 'dying' to be 'imbued' with new life. See commentary by the editor H. M. E. De Jong, 310–313.

Chapter 12

WORMHOLES IN THE LUCID VOID

Trust your dreams for in them you find the gate to eternity.[153]

— Khalil Gibran

In my lucid dreams, vortexes or tunnels spontaneously appear, seemingly out of nowhere, to ferry me at hyper-velocity to unknown destinations. For want of a better word, I have described these tunnels as 'wormholes'. One of my earliest such lucid dreams began like this:

I enter a room at twilight. There I teach English to a Frenchman. I am sitting on a bed, and he is on a chair next to me. As evening falls, the room darkens, and he becomes silhouetted in the diffused light. Softly he says in French, 'Ou es tu?' (Where are you?) I respond, 'Je suis ici' (I am here). As he leans forward to kiss me, I realise I am dreaming, at which moment it feels as if I am pulled between the man's lips into a long, dark, shining tunnel at an incredible speed. My dream body has disappeared, and I sense myself as a point of consciousness. To keep centred, I repeat a Holy Name. The 'wormhole' goes on and on and, spontaneously, I begin to sing a sacred hymn. As I sing, the velocity increases.

> *The journey abruptly ends in a silent space, where an iridescent darkness surrounds me. I wait, and a shimmer of light falls over me. I feel the presence of Spirit and wonder if these lights are angels. Then, without warning, I am being returned at an even greater speed, back through the same tunnel, as if guided by invisible Beings. When I awaken, it is 4 a.m.*

This initial experience bears the hallmarks of many wormhole dreams that were to follow:

1. The sudden appearance of the wormhole at a moment of focused concentration and profound feeling.
2. Primarily cylindrical forms that appear as vortexes, spheres or tunnels, with darkly luminescent interiors of varying inner construction, colours and movement.
3. The replacement of the 'dream body' with an awareness of an invisible, subtle body.
4. A powerful magnetic force that pulls the subtle body into the wormhole.
5. The sensation of being carried through the wormhole by a tremendous current of energy, requiring submission and concentrated focus to navigate.
6. Hyper-velocity transport through the wormhole that accelerates as devotional concentration deepens.
7. An abrupt ending that culminates in a gentle 'landing', stillness, and revelatory encounters at what seems to be a 'meeting' or 'viewing point'.
8. Unexpected and equally sudden reversal of the journey back through the wormhole, either to the original dream or to full waking consciousness.

As in the opening dream, a wormhole may form out of specific dream imagery, particularly lips, eyes and mirrors. When, in waking life or in a dream, we cross a threshold or a bridge, travel on transport or experience a rite of passage, we can think of ourselves as having taken a metaphorical 'wormhole' into a new dimension of consciousness, a new way of being. However, as I have become more confident in journeying through apparent wormholes, yet more massive and powerful vortices have arisen from within the Black Light of the lucid void. In this chapter, I shall attempt to describe the source, construction and purpose of these wormholes and to draw a comparison with reference to what we are now learning from advances in astrophysics.

When I first began encountering wormholes in dream lucidity in 2008, I knew only that physicists thought they may potentially create 'shortcuts' in space. Then, in 2014, at an international conference, when I was giving a talk on the phenomenology of my 'wormhole' dreams, fellow panellist and physicist Don Middendorf commented on how uncannily the descriptions of my lucid dream wormholes fitted with concepts of current astrophysics. Having since then delved into the science of wormholes, I now understand what my colleague meant! [154]

Lucid Surrender and Traversing Wormholes

The term 'wormhole' was coined in 1957 by physicists John Wheeler and Charles Misner to characterise a hypothetical 'bridge', postulated by Albert Einstein and Nathan Rosen in 1935, that could link distant domains of spacetime through hyperspace, on account of the fundamental curvature of spacetime.[155]

To illustrate how wormholes are thought to work, theoretical physicists use the image of a worm burrowing straight through an apple rather than going the longer way around the apple's surface, thereby taking a shorter route. The worm makes this journey by moving from the apple's three-dimensional surface through its interior, construed as a four-dimensional domain.

In recent years, the science of wormholes has gathered a pace. Black holes are now thought to be the 'mouths' of massive wormholes (a finding that tallies with my own observations in lucidity), while countless smaller, unstable wormholes are believed to appear and then disappear in the fabric of spacetime. However, in the physical universe, it is thought to be impossible for a person to survive travelling through such a wormhole, since the gravitational field would either stretch and crush the human body, or else the wormhole itself would collapse before it could be traversed.

After a good many 'wormhole' journeys in lucidity, I began to question the physicalist assumption that human beings would need some kind of spacecraft to travel through a wormhole. In Lucid Surrender, my experience has been that *a particular form of consciousness not only creates (or reveals) a wormhole but also makes traversing it possible*. Such wormholes generally appear in the lucid void in response to a feeling of gravitas — the deep state of concentration and devotion characteristic of Lucid Surrender.

One of my most powerful wormhole dreams, 'Saturnine Beings', which took place years after the dream that opens this chapter, illustrates this process. Characteristically, I prepare for such dreams by spending some time in prayer prior to falling sleep.[156] On this occasion, I woke up around four in the morning feeling upset about my work and personal life. I decided to say the 'Welcoming Prayer',[157] i.e. 'Welcome spitefulness, welcome resentment, welcome confusion, welcome unknowing, welcome desire…' Then a sung version of Psalm 28:7 welled up in me, 'You my God are my heart's desire':

The next moment, I realise that I am lucid, and my being is taken up on the Black Light, where I have the sensation of zigzagging back and forth for some time at great speed. It takes a lot of energy simply to keep my bearings. I start to ponder what all this is for. I feel terribly alone, but then remind myself that celestial Beings surround me. After some time, I recall the song from my prayers before sleep: 'You my God are my heart's desire, and my soul cries out to Thee. You my God are my strength, my shield, to you oh Lord will your Servant yield. You my God are my heart's desire, and my soul cries out to Thee.'

As the song continues, I have the distinct impression that my very being curls up and takes refuge in the words and music like a butterfly in a cocoon. Encapsulated in this way, my soul is pulled into a wormhole funnel at incredible velocity. The intensity of the journey begins to feel unbearable. I call out, 'I wish I could see you, Holy Beings of Light.' At that moment, my essence 'splashes' into a pool of shimmering pinpricks of living lights. Before me, a stunning, endless expanse of new planets and constellations is revealed.

A group of five planets of massive proportions cluster

together in front of me in a most unusual way, leaning into one another like friends or family consulting one another. They emit a striking, tawny-coloured light. I notice that these great planets have Saturnine rings around them, which tilt with their movements. The overall impression is one of serene equanimity combined with fiery intensity and intelligence, causing me to wonder whether these planets are actually Great Beings.

The clear beauty, piercing intelligence, and the tremendous force of the scene startles me, and as my internal focus shifts, I am pulled back through the wormhole passage, feeling disappointed that I couldn't stay there longer, yet grateful to have been shown such a vista within Lucid Surrender.

Over recent years, physicists have extended the wormhole analogy, hypothesising that deep within the 'core' of hyperspace, space-time as we know it may give way to multiple dimensions, [158] where other worlds invisible to us may exist. Wormholes could, in theory, enable us to enter these dimensions. Furthermore, the physicist John Hagelin has argued that, at the quantum level, the entire universe arises from a 'unified field of consciousness'. [159] In Hagelin's view, wormholes allow for the creation of midway points where different points within the same universe can meet. Based on my experience of wormholes, I have wondered if they connect different dimensions in the multiverse.

Correspondingly, in my lucid dreams, there has always felt to be an interplay between my consciousness and wormhole phenomena, in which my devotional gravitas on one side of the wormhole transports me to extra-dimensional

Beings on the other side. It seems the energy of my consciousness becomes the vehicle required for traversing the wormhole, my focus and desire has been greeted by a greater, transpersonal presence from beyond.

Sustaining Wormholes in Lucidity

In the dream 'Saturnine Beings', I realised that my *state of mind* was the key to travelling *through* the wormhole. A year later I had another wormhole dream — an excerpt from which follows — in which it came to me that my conscious awareness is actually instrumental in the *creation* of the wormhole:

> *After a long period of prayer, I dream and become lucid. For the first time, my being is taken through a field of octagonal structures made of light filaments whose beauty mesmerises me. Eventually, the abstract forms give way to a tunnel about the width of my extended arms (although, at this point, I no longer have a visible, physical body).*
>
> *As I am pulled into the wormhole, I note that the spinning sides look to be made of a shiny Black Light that appears 'wet'. I exclaim, 'A wormhole!' I wonder where this wormhole leads me. For the first time, I become aware that my consciousness somehow creates this wormhole, and I am anxious that it might collapse should my concentration give way. Just when I think my fear will overwhelm me, the tunnel opens up into a still, black, quiet space. I become aware of a Holy presence…*

Two years later, during a lucid dream, I became aware of how my conscious awareness not only *creates* the wormhole but also helps to *sustain* it:

I am on the Black Light in the lucid void. As I sing 'The Lord's Prayer', an amazing wormhole passage opens up — an immense, webbed, lattice-like structure, with a square perimeter and supported within by what appear to be many arched beams, as in the vault of a cathedral roof or the ribs lining the hull of a great wooden ship, only that here the 'beams' look made of a fluid substance.

As I pray, I feel myself carried by two invisible Beings. The deeper the prayer, the faster we go. The unseen Beings carry me backwards, so I cannot see where I am headed, but only where I have been while the wormhole rises up around me like a cresting wave that never collapses.

After some time, I wonder what will happen if I'm woken up while in the wormhole. Will I find myself in a deranged mental state? But upon hearing the same words that I have heard in other wormholes, 'You are safe,' I decide not to worry. The movement begins to slow, 'Will I see another world? Meet Holy Beings?'

As the movement stops altogether, my subtle body is lowered so that my invisible feet touch down. This time it feels as if I am placed in a pool of bubbling Black Light, that moves up from the soles of my feet and rises with a surge of intense, joyful life. The Divine touching me in this sweet way reminds me of Jesus washing the feet of his disciples to show that he was also their servant and friend.

Some years after this dream, when reading research on wormholes, I was intrigued to find a diagram illustrating the effects of a spacecraft travelling at 'warp drive' through a wormhole, thus creating a 'bubble of asymmetrical spacetime curvature' around the spacecraft, akin to the formation in my dream.[160]

The wormhole as a portal to a meeting place in the realm of the transpersonal is foregrounded in a lucid dream I had during the Covid-19 pandemic in 2020. There I met, for the second time, a Being that had appeared fourteen years earlier, as a 'Black Sun' (see Chapter Six). Prior to falling asleep, I had prayed for guidance and support in living through the pandemic.

I am surprised to find myself on an island where the buildings are painted crisp white and azure blue as in Greece. The beauty of the scene makes me aware that I am dreaming! I pause to see what happens and am abruptly pulled into a 'wormhole' of incredible depth that looks like a great rotating whirlwind of Black Light. Falling downwards, I sing the hymn 'How Great Thou Art'. The descent lasts until I have nearly finished the hymn's first verse, and I begin to think, 'What next?'

The movement slows and stops, and I am 'flipped over' onto my belly. I float there in space somewhat surprised to see, just a foot away from me, a massive spherical disc of shining Black Light, whose edges radiate an intense white light, like a solar eclipse. 'Ah,' I think. 'The Black Sun. We meet again.'

There follows a long silence between us until, spontaneously, I bow my head slightly and silently ask, 'How can I best serve?' With this, two slits of piercing white light open up like eyes on the sphere's surface, converging into one that hits me between my eyebrows, then bouncing back and forth across my brow. After a while, I raise my left hand to the light, and with my shift in focus, I am pulled back through the wormhole. I wake up feeling tired but expansive, my forehead still zinging.

The two lines of light that appeared on the radiating Black Sun reminded me of quantum theory's double slit experiment.

No explicit guidance was given, yet the Black Sun's light instilled me with the will, hope, wonder and love needed to engage with whatever the pandemic should bring. The answer to my prayerful request to the Black Sun, 'How can I best serve?', came through empowering and emboldening me for the writing on Lucid Surrender that lay ahead.

The Mysterious Properties of Wormholes

I have long puzzled over the psycho-spiritual challenges presented by my lucid encounters with wormholes. Sometimes, it seems to me that the powerful spinning, pulsating or zigzagging movement of the wormholes acts as a kind of purification process, like a great washing machine, that churns, cleanses and finally stills the mind. Other times, it feels as though the wormhole is challenging my capacity to stay present to the unknown and to what I may meet at the wormhole's end. Notably, I have never awakened direct from within the wormhole — the dream narrative must find completion.

Most wormholes have had the appearance of wet obsidian illuminated by moonlight. Many reverberate with geometric traceries of vibrant light against radiant darkness, primarily hexagons, octagonal patterns, parabolic structures or ribbed vaulting. Whatever shape it takes feels alive with intelligent intent.

Some wormholes have flashed throughout with a kaleidoscope of blurring colours. A few shine with one dominant colour. In one instance, I think, 'Oh the green! This is the Spirit! This is the "greening"!' The green gives me hope. Sometimes, the colours seen in the wormhole presage the resplendence of the journey's end, the world to which I am being taken, as in this dream:

I am in a room where I hold a dream group. Opposite me, a wall covers the door of a large closet. As I become lucid, my being gets pulled through the mirror into a black and grey swirling vortex — a wormhole! It feels as if I have entered a massive accelerator at a tremendous speed. The Lord's Prayer comes to mind and sings in me the entire way.

Eventually the movement slows and beneath me I see a stream of brightly coloured forms and patterns. After passing through the wormhole, I pop into a populated landscape.

I realise that the colours I had seen in the wormhole were from this place but that until this moment I had been viewing them as if through water. The terrain is very beautiful, harmonious, and intensely coloured. I wonder if I have actually come to another planet, as light radiates from within its forms.

When travelling through wormholes, I have wondered if the speed is superluminal, faster than light. In one lucid dream, I managed to ask the Being, who carried me through the wormhole, how fast we had been travelling. He replied casually, '500,000 *miles per second.*' Given that I had sung the entire Lord's Prayer while passing through the wormhole, we must have travelled far indeed! However, I have never managed to clarify just *where* I have been taken. When the unknown and unnamed destination is reached, it has the feeling of being both nowhere and somewhere, a locale beyond the parameters of spacetime.

An anecdote from my life comes to mind. Once, when I was on an airport bus travelling from Stansted to London, the bus pulled over unexpectedly and waited there for some time. Two tourists sitting behind me became impatient and began to argue over where the bus actually was. 'How can the bus stop in the middle of nowhere?' asked the woman. 'This is not a nowhere,' replied the man. 'This is a somewhere; buses don't stop at a nowhere.' Then the bus started moving again, passing by a sign, and the man read out repeatedly, 'North Watford, North Watford, North Watford.' 'I heard you already,' said his partner, 'but what does that *mean*?' The man answered, 'It means that this is a somewhere, because North Watford is not a nowhere; it is a somewhere.' Similarly, where the wormhole leads, while seemingly 'nowhere', is paradoxically experienced by me as the most absolute 'somewhere'.

The Return

After having spent time on one side of the wormhole, the return 'home' usually comes unexpectedly and involves a reversal of the journey back through the wormhole at warp-speed. For instance, after re-emerging from a wormhole I often find myself back in the original dream still lucid, resting full length on what might be a yoga mat, bed, or beach, depending on the initial dreamscape. This gives me an opportunity to recover from the journey before I awake fully. Other times, I may tumble out of the wormhole, somersaulting abruptly into a dream through a mirror or another image that serves as a re-entry point.

Often upon my return to the original dream, I have been met by a dream Being. One time, a Tibetan Buddhist monk greeted me and explained that such dreams build up the dreamer's capacity to enter the unknown. I also recall being met by a youthful man who took me in his arms and kissed me with great force as if to congratulate me on my successful transit of the wormhole. On another occasion, a man came up to me and said that it was important to share such dreams — guidance I have followed. Such encounters give the journey a sense of completion and purpose.

Once, after travelling through a wormhole in a lucid dream, I asked silently, 'Why all this, the forms of light, the wormhole, the Black Light and Beings of Light?' The unseen presence in the dream replied quietly and simply, 'Because you need filling.' This reply left me feeling humbled and grateful. After this dream, I realised that wormholes also connect us, like great umbilical cords, to the very source of life.[161]

Notes:

153. This teaching has been a touchstone for me. Khalil Gibran, *The Prophet* (New York, NY: Alfred A. Knopf, 1951), 71.
154. Subsequently, when I read *The Truth in the Light: An Investigation of over 300 Near-Death Experiences* by Peter and Elizabeth Fenwick (London: Headline Book Publishing, 1995), I noticed that the wormhole phenomena

of my lucid dreams share many similarities with the 'tunnels' that lead to the 'light', as reported in Near Death Experiences.
155. C. W. Misner, J. A. Wheeler, 'Classical physics as geometry', *Annals of Physics*, 2, No. 6 (1957): 525, doi:10.1016/0003-4916(57)90049-0
156. Before sleep, I often sing 'The Lord's Prayer' to whatever tune comes to mind. This might be a hymn, a melody from the classical repertoire or a popular song such as 'Somewhere over the Rainbow' or even, 'Blue Moon'. Once I become lucid and my soul is taken into the void, this sung prayer (or another sacred song), spontaneously arises. For long journeys, 'The Lord's Prayer' has helped me to sustain lucidity, especially when it involves wormhole or Black Light transit.
157. For a more in-depth look at this form of prayer, see Chapter 13, 'The Welcoming Prayer', in Cynthia Bourgeault's *Centering Prayer and Inner Awakening* (Cambridge, Massachusetts: Cowley Publishing, 2004), 135–152.
158. The Nobel Prize-winning physicist Kip S. Thorne gives a fascinating and accessible account of the science of such phenomena in his book, *Black Holes & Time Warps: Einstein's Outrageous Legacy* (New York and London: W. W. Norton & Company, 1994).
159. For an elaboration of this theory see John Hagelin's 'Entanglement, Space-Time Wormholes, and the Brain', *Science and Nonduality Series*, 5 December 2014, https://www.youtube.com/watch?v=nvVDYQoGWyk.
160. Theoretically, 'warp drive' allows for travelling faster than the speed of light. The type of structure such warp-speed travel would cause is called an 'Alcubierre "top-hat" metric'. See Richard K. Obousy's and Gerald Cleaver's paper, 'Putting the "Warp" Back into Warp Drive', *Spaceflight*, 50, No. 4 (April 2008): Figure 2, arXiv:0807.1957v2 [physics.pop-ph]
161. My thanks to Christine Anderson for suggesting that the wormhole can be likened to the birth canal. (Personal communication at the 'ManyWorlds of Lucid Dreaming Online Conference' November 12, 2021). Her observation reminds me of Stanislov Grof's pioneering work with therapeutic doses of LSD and his description of the perinatal matrices of the birth canal re-experienced in psychedelic therapy. See his ground-breaking work, *Beyond the Brain: Birth, Death, and Transcendence in Psychotherapy* listed in the Bibliography.

CELESTIAL DREAM TIGERS

Part IV

LIGHT, LOVE AND LAUGHTER IN LUCID SURRENDER

*God placed sleep in the animate world
only so that everyone might witness
the Presence of Imagination
and know that there is another world
similar to the sensory world.*

— Ibn al-'Arabi [162] (12th-century Sufi mystic)

Chapter 13

MOVING FROM CONDITIONED REALITY TO THE FREEDOM OF HEART[163]

It is not ethical principles, however lofty, or creeds, however orthodox, that lay the foundations for the freedom and autonomy of the individual, but simply and solely the empirical awareness, the incontrovertible experience of an intensely personal, reciprocal relationship between man and an extramundane authority which acts as a counterpoise to the 'world' and its 'reason'.[164]

— Carl Jung

You really are brainwashed, aren't you?' — these words were spoken by a dream Being who said this to me when, because of my scruples, I turned down his invitation in the dream to 'love and desire' him. Upon reflection, his words woke me up to a new way of thinking about how I respond to invitations from dream Beings that possess transpersonal attributes such as wisdom, beauty, truth, harmony, might, mercy, mystery, love and compassion.

In this case, the Being that spoke to me appeared as a striking Native American. Here is the complete dream, which

I had early on in my experience of dream lucidity during my first marriage:

> *I go out of the flat where I live to get some air on a clear night, ending up at a nearby petrol station. As I mill around, a man approaches me. Initially, I confuse him with my former lover. But then I see that he is a man that I know and love but do not recognise fully, a Native American with straight, shiny black hair. He stands before me tall, slim and fit, his body quivering with intelligence and desire.*
>
> *He walks up to me purposively and faces me. He is crying, and I notice his tears are like moonbeams or dewdrops full of light. He tells me, 'It's hard to love you so and see the light in your bedroom but not share it with you.' He says, 'You were working at that "shit" school for so long and so busy it's no wonder you didn't have children with me.' He seems full of righteous indignation. I say defensively, 'Well then I bet you're sorry that we met at that school.' He calms down and says, 'Of course I'm not sorry we met there. I love you.' But I am aware that I am married, and I say to him, 'How can I look upon you with love and desire?' Then he turns to me and says, 'You really are brainwashed, aren't you!' As he sadly turns away, I realise I have missed an opportunity to meet what Sufis call the 'lover' aspect of the Divine, but, instead of becoming fully lucid, I wake up with that awareness, feeling impatient with myself.*

In retrospect, if I had dwelt upon the other-worldly tears he cried as he spoke to me — a magical detail signalling the presence of the transpersonal — rather than my fears, then

I would have been more able to receive what he was truly offering me. If I had accepted his invitation, this encounter might have potentially knocked me out of my conventional morality into a fuller understanding of my own heart. Since this dream, I have sought a more receptive position towards requests from such transpersonal dream figures, realising that they seek to open our hearts and minds, not only for our own benefit but for the benefit of others as well.

With hindsight, I see more clearly how my dreams have invited and instructed me to become a 'consenting adult', while challenging me to move beyond my conditioned view of reality in order to enter into a more intimate and unitive relationship with the dream as it unfolds and, in turn, with waking life. When both the dreamer and the dream say, 'I do!', then it is as though the transpersonal reality is announcing, 'You may kiss the bride!'

Alchemists refer to such a sense of unity as a 'royal wedding', the union of the soul — the essence of the individual — and Spirit. Kabbalists describe this union as the mystic marriage; Christians, as the marriage of the lamb; and in Greco-Roman culture, the marriage of the gods, or *hierosgamos*. What aspects of our being 'marry' in our psyches? To paraphrase Carl Jung's description of what he experienced in the visionary dreams he had towards the end of his life, 'At the bottom it is our very selves: We are the marriage. And our beatitude is that of a blissful wedding.' [165]

Sometimes, as in my case, our dreams may have to court us for a long time before we may feel ready, within a dream, to let go of our limited, waking-world caution and to say 'Yes!'

wholeheartedly to the intimacy offered by the dream. Doing so brings a deepening of lucidity, freeing us to act with more awareness and choice. In the course of lucid dreaming, as we become more aware of the mental attitudes and concepts shaping our perceptions and reactions, we can learn to move beyond the limitations of the conditioned mind and recognise the guidance the dream provides.

I recall having a dream that illustrates the emergence of this awareness in lucidity, one in which I am coaxed into recognition of my essential soul nature.

Entering an unfamiliar building, I become lucid. Great joy fills me. Holy black winds carry me inwards to a place of stillness. Far off in the distance, moving shapes of colour approach me. They look like massive, magical butterflies of deep blues, greens, purples, yellows and reds outlined in black. The coloured spots on their wings shine like jewels. They surround me and caress me with their coloured wings. Their touch feels full of grace, beauty and intelligence. They lead me into a large hall that appears decorated in colours echoing their peacock-coloured wings.

A beautiful woman gets up to greet me. We communicate without words. She shows me the treasures in the room as if to introduce me to what already feels mine. Then she picks up a finely wrought, wreath-shaped crown of delicate leaves with four slim golden bands crossing at the top. I am dazzled by the crown's shining beauty and delicate power. As she moves to set it upon my head, I recoil, aware that I am no king nor queen. Undeterred, she continues to lower the crown onto my head, saying, 'This is the Holy Spirit.' Hearing this, I become more able to accept the gift. When the crown touches my head, a shower of powerful emotion overcomes me, washes down through me, and pulls me again into the bright blackness that gently lifts me to waking consciousness.

My initial reaction to this coronation, in which I contract from the interaction, illustrates the confining nature of conditional reality, in which our self-limiting views, feelings of unworthiness or shame or even arrogance and pride, keep us from accepting the gifts conferred by both dreams and life itself. Happily, in this case, the beauty and gentleness of the woman in the dream reassured me, enabling me to overcome my own self-doubts.

Even when my own narrow adherence to my past conditioning dominates in a lucid dream, causing me to act 'brainwashed', I have learned to become aware of this limitation, being mindful of what the transpersonal archetypal realm can open up to us, as shown in this scene from a lucid dream:

After crossing a black expanse of light and abstract forms, I find myself spinning round in the centre of a large, fantastically coloured hall. I see walls and sloping ceilings covered with paintings that look alive with moving pictures. A couple sits viewing them. Startled by my entrance, the woman gets up and approaches me. She looks very fine and moves like a graceful sprite. Her skin shines with a blue hue and her lips radiate a bluish, white, laser light, capturing my attention.

With delicate determination, she says to me, 'What part

of my dream are you?' The implications of her question amaze and frighten me. Rather than responding thoughtfully, I say flippantly the first thing that comes to mind: *'Your blue lips.'* My attitude clearly hurts the woman. I ask her in turn, *'And what part of my dream are you?'* She responds in kind, saying, *'Your small breasts.' 'Ouch!'* I think. *'I guess I deserved that.'*

The intense colours and strange beauty of the scene begin to feel oppressive to me and I wonder if I can get out of this place at will or whether I'll be stuck here and go mad. With this, I open my eyes curious to know how it will feel to come back so rapidly to waking reality. I find myself lying in bed, feeling dismayed at my behaviour. My heart sends the blue lady a heartfelt apology and the wish that I may one day meet her again. I sense that she also probably feels disappointed in our encounter.

Although, in this case, I didn't respond to the blue lady in a way that could develop our encounter, it does strike me as important that she and I both agreed we had found ourselves in a realm known through dreams, one in which we might have conversed soulfully and with great depth of meaning. I haven't as yet encountered this dream Being again, yet I suspect she may have made an appearance since in other guises.

In Lucid Surrender, when I leave my dream body behind, or rather, find it stripped away, my soul is carried across expanses of Black Light and drawn into a light form that acts as a passage into another dream dimension, where a new dream body often emerges. Over time, I have realised that my new dream body may appear differently from that of non-lucid dreams, for example, outlined in light only or of a shining black. Regardless of my appearance, the dream Beings greet me in such a way that it feels as though they would like to enter into relationship with me.

For example, one time, after crossing the Lucid Void, I tumble through space before somersaulting onto a hexagonal platform. A young boy comes by and, seeing me, calls out to his father, 'Hey, Dad, come look at this!', as if he doesn't seem quite certain of what to make of me or where I have come from, but he is clearly curious. That sets me wondering how I appear. In another dream, after I get pulled into a dream-mirror, carried across the Black Light, and into a geometric light form, I pop into a dreamscape reminiscent of my childhood. There, women who appear both earthy and angelic come out and stroke my new dream body with their hands as if, by doing so, they receive some knowledge through me. At the same time, I feel aware of receiving some kind of blessing through the women's hands.

When travelling on the Black Light, I notice that the apparent void seems to read my thoughts, often a voice or thought-form coming forward to reassure me and bring me round to a new way of being. For instance, if I feel afraid to enter a light form, a voice might say, 'Come into my being,' or if I feel unsafe, I may hear a reassuring, 'You are safe.' Once, when I felt tempted to lose myself in the ecstatic sensation of the Black Light, a clear voice said, 'It's not this!', reminding me to keep my focus for the next part of the journey.

In such ways, the dreams help me to overcome my childish obstinacy or fearfulness and to behave more like a consenting adult, as I respond to a greater wisdom. For example, sometimes, out of the blackness, an invisible hand may emerge to direct me, gently pushing my own hands together in prayer, a position that accelerates my journey on the black winds. At other times, an invisible hand may gently stop me from undertaking an action, as in the following dream:

> *With the onset of lucidity, I feel the tug of wind, but it feels hard to release myself to the infinite blackness. Finally, I call out, 'Take me to you, God!' With this the release comes and my soul is lifted onto the powerful winds. The blackness lights up as a white beam of light darts towards me and loops once around my neck powerfully. The force at the base of my throat feels so great at one point I raise my invisible hand to loosen it, but then I feel my hand pushed down lightly so as to allow the force to have its way, and for me to accept it as a kind of opening.*

Sometimes, when I have sought to impose my personal will in a lucid dream, the dream has reminded me of the need for humility, as in this encounter:

> *In the night, I wake up and pray. Soon, I hear a whirring sound and then, against the backdrop of blackness, there appears a full moon so beautiful it makes me weep. My soul rises up and moves into the glittering darkness with great joy. At some point, I become aware that I am being carried by a rod-like Being of light running down my midriff. But I feel so taken with the delight, my mind thinks to let go of this beam of light and to plunge into the blackness. As I abruptly move to do so, I am pulled back by my ankles, and I immediately realise my*

error. The dignity of this Being of light hits me hard. I bow my head and say, 'Forgive me, Holy Being,' and I hear the words, 'You are forgiven.' With this, we lift off again and soar like birds high on the edge of the winds. A deep ecstasy runs through me, yet I cannot somehow surrender fully. I awake surprised to find myself under the covers.

At other times, the dream has made it clear that the shift from personal lucidity to transpersonal lucidity will only come about through surrender of the ego, as in this dream:

In lucidity, I go to a nearby window and open it. Feeling rather empty inside, I dive out in an off-hand, cold manner, thinking that it's only a dream in any case. Instead of trying to fly, I wait rather imperiously for the Spirit to come for me. After falling for what seems an unusually long time into the black, I recall Satan tempting Jesus to leap off a cliff only to have God's angels come to save him. Jesus refused, saying, 'Thou shall not tempt the Lord thy God.' 'Well, God,' I think, 'I didn't mean it quite like that.' Then the winds take hold of me and carry me into the Black Light.

Finally, I break through the black into an intense field of blinding blue light, like breaking through to the surface from the depths of the sea. 'The blue!' I think, feeling reassured. Although the blue in other dreams has been breath-taking, this blue seems by far the most dazzling of all, almost diamond white to my eyes. My Soul feels seared and cleansed by the light, which takes some time to cross.

There comes a descent into blackness, and, against this

backdrop luminous darkness, I see an immense black whirlwind, seemingly composed of layered veils of black lace with moonlight shining through. Taken into the centre of this cloud, my soul knows that I am at the very centre of things, in God's embrace. The lacy forms in the whirlwind look amazingly intricate and exquisite, yet simple and beautiful. Their beauty is irresistible, and I lift my right hand to touch the patterns. Doing so fills me with great joy, unbounded trust, and a profound knowing. The lacy pattern reads like a hieroglyph for life, and, for some time, I feel shrouded in a wonderful mysterious love.

Over time, I have learned that aligning my will with that of the dreams from a heart-centred position opens up far more than I could have ever imagined. Nonetheless, dream Beings have made it clear to me that I generally have a choice about how I behave in a dreamscape and that this choice will shape the transpersonal ramifications of the dream, as illustrated here:

In the dream, I go outside a classroom where a massive black dog, with thick black curls, comes up to greet me. As it occurs to me that no such kind of dog exists in actuality, I become lucid. I am aware that in daily life I've been very stressed and my prayers unfocused, so I hadn't expected to receive a lucid dream. Even so, I bow my head, and all falls away into blackness. The ecstasy grips me, and, moving through this, I repeat, 'O Holy One!'

I feel carried some distance on refreshing winds into a wide hall with high open windows through which the sunlight streams and a gentle breeze billows through white curtains.

> *Women, wearing high-waisted, long gowns in solid red, green, yellow or blue lined with gold brocade, sing beautiful hymns to God. As they sing, they walk meditatively round the hall while I am carried to a far corner where a small door in the wall opens, and a man's face and hands appear. He holds a thin rod made of braided silver, on the end of which is set a fine ruby. I feel he wants to insert this into my left nostril, up into the space between my eyes. The thought repels and frightens me until one of the women says, 'You have a choice,' and I know I can decide whether to wake up and leave the experience or stay in it.*
>
> *Because the scene, music, rod and ruby look so beautiful, even though I am apprehensive, I determine not to fight but to receive what appears to be some kind of 'implant'. As I do so, I keep repeating, 'Oh Holy One.' My being is carried a great distance through the blackness into a further dream in which a dream figure says with great surprise, 'What has happened to you?' I find it significant that he has intuited a change in me. Then I actually do wake up.*

Other times, however, a dream character will suggest to me that the choice in a dream is not always up to me alone, even in lucidity, as in this dream excerpt:

> *When the descent on the Black Light ends, I find myself with a dream body standing erect and facing a lovely woman who holds each of my hands in her own. Wrapped around her body and head, she wears a satin blue veil with an embroidered gold trim. Only her stunning, dark eyes are visible, above a diaphanous white veil with a woman's face painted on it*

covering her own. The portrait reminds me of myself. I say to her, 'So you are my guide this time.'

She takes me through a door that opens from the black in a white room that looks like an operating theatre and explains, 'I'm here to stop your soul from dying, or at least to make sure that your soul re-incarnates.' My mind wants to ask what she means about my dying. Does she mean now or later? A pang rises up in my heart, and though I don't recall a single detail of my former earthly life, its sorrows and joys flood through me, and I say aloud, 'I'm not so sure I want to re-incarnate, even if it's possible.' But she smiles and says, 'Given what your soul knows, it may have to do so.' I then allow her to carry out a surgical procedure on me, which I believe would be beneficial.

Following this dream, I became ill with stomach pains. Reflecting on the experience, I understood the surgery within the dream as unblocking negative feelings that I had been holding in my body. I was also forcibly reminded that, as the dream suggests, I will ultimately have no choice but to surrender to death and what is to follow. Yet such dreams have taught me that in death, as in life, we are never alone, and that we are, all of us, loved. In response to this awareness of deeply felt love, the dreams ask only for our wholehearted 'Yes!'

Notes:

162. Cited by Chittick, *Imaginal Worlds*, 26.
163. Originally published as 'Beyond the Matrix: From Consensus Reality to Heart Consciousness' in *Lucid Dreaming Experience*, 2, No. 1 (June 2013): 20–27.
164. Carl Jung, *The Undiscovered Self*, 4th edition, trans. R. F. C. Hull (London: Routledge & Kegan Paul, 1958, 1969), 23.
165. Carl Jung, *Memories, Dreams, Reflections*, ed. Aniela Jaffé, trans. Richard and Clara Winston (New York: Random House, 1965), 294.

Chapter 14

THE GENTLE HUMOUR OF LUCIDITY [166]

*But the angels come back and laugh in my dreams,
I wonder what it means.* [167]

— Judee Sill

Now and again, angels laugh in my dreams. I believe they do so to show me how to have a lighter heart and mind. Such dreams remind me of the Biblical Proverb, 'A happy heart is good medicine, and a cheerful mind works healing, but a broken spirit dries up the bones.' [168] Dreams act as soul-medicine that sometimes is taken more easily with humour. I get the sense that they employ their own kind of comic relief to overcome the stubbornness of my ego.

Such humorous coaxing has occurred in many forms, leaving me to ponder what it all means. For example, consider this semi-lucid dream that I had in 2008:

I walk with Bob Dylan by the sea under a starlit sky. As we walk along, I ruffle his hair and call him a little nihilist. He asks me what a theist is, so I explain how a theist believes there is a God but that such a God doesn't take personal interest in human affairs. And then I ask, 'What's a sophist?' and he says, 'An asshole!' and we laugh. 'There is another type,' I say. Pressing my hands to my temples, I try to come up with the word, but it escapes me. I only know it is a word for those who love wisdom that has more positive connotations. I look up at the stars — something that normally brings lucidity — but the repartee and focus on the words distracts me, and I awaken.

While a dream Being may say something humorous, I have noted that sometimes the dreamscape itself sets the stage for gentle comedy. For instance, in the following lucid dream, which I had some years after the previous one, I am shown my mental block in a very literal way. At the same time, the dream provides me with its own touching consolation:

Black Light and winds carry my being into the void. This comes with such a blissful feeling that I get somewhat distracted in wondering how to make this feeling last. Soon after, my (now invisible) dream body screeches to a halt a fraction of an inch in front of an obsidian-like wall that reaches beyond my vision in either direction.

Like in a slapstick comedy, I slide down, along the height of the wall, to the ground. There, I find myself with a dream body looking up at the towering barrier. Sadness comes over me as I realise that I have not been able, or perhaps allowed, to continue because I had not simply trusted my heart to take me where I needed to go.

As I turn away from the wall, a garden appears, and I lie down near a lovely, large pink flower. I feel tired so I say to the flower, 'Please come to me.' To my surprise, it does so, walking on its roots. Then it leans over, caressing me with one of its petals. With this, I am infused with the sweetness and gentleness of its being.

From time to time, sweetly comic figures have appeared in the lucid dreams acting as guides, as in this dream two years on:

Just before waking, I find myself resting in a bed within a dream and realise that the people around me wouldn't be there if I were truly asleep. This awareness brings lucidity. I feel happy on the one hand and apprehensive on the other because of my confused state of mind. The dreamscape falls away and my being remains static in the Black Light.

To my delight, a little green, Jiminy Cricket-type creature comes up to me. He puts his arms over his head, palms together, demonstrating what I need to do. I smile, inwardly feeling both charmed and curious about this little creature. I mirror his posture, and with this movement, ecstasy fills me. Eventually, the black opens up to immense white rings of light set amidst the dark expanse. I stop to ponder these lights until the Jiminy Cricket fellow appears again and beckons me on with his little green arm and large, white-gloved hand, pulling, or rather, willing me along as the dream continues to unfold.

Another time, a little bird, hopping to and fro, was to show me the way. This dream took place when I was going through a divorce and so had asked for dream guidance before falling asleep:

> *In the dream, I find myself thinking, 'Now you know this is a dream,' and so become lucid. But I am worried because I feel exposed, somehow not shielded by the Holy Spirit. My being is carried through a field of pulsating white light, followed by a steep and long descent.*
>
> *I end up in a scene next to a cartoon-like little bird that appears very tired, with its wings hanging down listlessly. I realise it is weary from carrying me, though I can't imagine how such a small bird could do so. To encourage the little fellow, I say, 'Thank you, Holy bird, for carrying me.' With this the bird revives and hops about, bringing my attention to what appears before us. We seem positioned in a kind of viewing terrace or box at the opera, and below a scene plays out in response to my request for guidance.*

Occasionally in a lucid dream, angelic laughter has given me a much needed lightness of being. Such laughter seems to flow over me gently with tender humour. Here is an example that I had about the time of the previous dream, again after asking for guidance:

> *Waking up in the night, I pray. There comes a shift, and I see intense colours before me and realise I am dreaming. The black winds seize me, and I am taken on a descent through a vortex. Eventually the speed slows. As I 'touch down', I feel the familiar sensation of cool, delightful sands on the soles of my feet as they*

become a conduit for all the goodness and beauty of the Holy sands.

Then an invisible Being picks me up and, carrying me low to the ground, circles counter-clockwise. I lean over towards the ground, running my fingers playfully through sands, like a rake making lines in a Zen rock garden. The winds whip around me playfully, yet powerfully, faster and faster, stirring up the sands as my fingertips make deeper furrows. 'What can this be for?' I wonder.

In the midst of this motion, my being pops into a space before what I think must be the throne of God — a white edifice studded with colourful jewels. I see that beyond are jewel-like rooms or halls, richly decorated and furnished in deep red, blue, green, purple and gold. The rooms are filled with books and angelic Beings who mill about reading and conversing.

The Holy place seems to contain all knowledge, like an endless library, and all love, expressed in the beautiful way the angelic Beings there relate. The thought that this form has been made by the whirling motion and the movement of my fingers in the sands flashes across my consciousness and hits me hard. 'No,' I think, 'that can't be!' And then I hear a soft, tinkling laughter that I have heard before in lucidity, and realise that it comes from a chorus of angelic, female voices calling out to me using my childhood nickname with bemusement, 'What do we have to do for Mindy to change?', as if no matter what they conjure up for me, I remain impervious. Yet, like a patient lover, the angels await the beloved's response.

Such commentary in my dreams generally has the quality of chiming bells or cymbals, as in this further lucid dream:

In the night, I wake up and pray. In the midst of my prayers, I find myself on the black winds. Then I am gently set down in the centre of a courtyard before a grand building, over which colourful banners fly. I sit on the grass in the courtyard. Women and men walk gracefully around, wearing colourful, flowing gowns and capes.

A fairy-like woman kneels down and pours out a handful of capsules into the palm of her hand and then onto the grass. I have no doubt I should take these, so I take one that looks half blue and half black and try to swallow it. The pill catches in my throat and begins to dissolve. I fear I'll choke. Realising that is just a fear that my mind is holding, I think how much I would love a glass of water, and, to my surprise, one appears in my hand. But, doubting the water could be real, I then find that the water doesn't help. I feel frustrated and confused.

Again, my soul is taken up by the winds and carried for some time before I find myself re-deposited in the centre of the same courtyard again with a dream body. Immediately, I fall to my knees to search for the capsules, realising I have been given a second chance. When I find a capsule, it turns into a silver ring with a large aquamarine stone. Recalling the other capsules, I begin to search for them. But how will I find them amidst the blades of grass? Instantly, four similar rings appear, all silver with large, sky-blue crystal stones, each with a slightly different cut. The capsules have all changed to rings, five altogether, one for each finger of my left hand.

Then my soul rises up as the winds whisk me out of the courtyard. As I look back, I see that gates of gold have opened to release me onto a field of Black Light. Behind them towers a fantastical silvery castle shining out from against the black backdrop. I feel preoccupied with thinking, 'How can I possibly describe its beauty?', when I hear pleasant, tinkling laughter and a lovely, light, feminine voice calling out to me, 'Remember where you come from.' On hearing this, and light of heart, my soul is carried far on the Black Light before re-entering my body.

Dreams like these, with their gentle, teasing humour, can lovingly help us to 'Remember where we come from' — that is, the birthplace of the soul wherein arises all of existence. Sometimes, the truth of a dream can be hard to swallow! Yet, in the end, thanks not least to a draught of lucid love and humour, the soul-medicine of our dreams finds its way to our heart.

Notes:

166. Originally published as 'Love's Lucid Labours Nearly Lost', in *Lucid Dreaming Experience*, 2, No. 4 (March 2014): 13–15.
167. From 'Crayon Angel', on *Crayon Angel: A Tribute to the Music of Judee Sill*, American Dust, 1971, compact disc.
168. Proverb 17:22, Amplified Bible.

Chapter 15

THE SACRED SANDS OF LUCID SURRENDER [169]

To see a World in a Grain of Sand... [170]

— William Blake

How do we remain open to surrender in lucidity? Over many years, I have had the chance to explore the response to this question experientially in many lucid dreams. Consequently, I have written at some length about Lucid Surrender and given many talks on the subject. Yet, none of this means I can offer a definitive framework. On the contrary, the more I think I know, the greater the expanse of the unknown. Instead, I will simply offer up some further reflections about the nature of Lucid Surrender before concluding with two dreams in response to my opening question.

In the English language, 'I surrender' implies both agency and will, a paradox in which one wilfully surrenders! Perhaps unsurprisingly, the more I wilfully attempt to surrender, the less I can do so. Romance languages suggest a more mysterious understanding of surrender. For example, a literal translation from the French would be, 'I am surrendered' or 'I surrender to myself.'

Lucid dreamers often ask me, 'To whom or what do I surrender?' But we might equally ask ourselves, 'Who or what is the "I" that surrenders?'

Words from St Thomas Aquinas, as rendered by the poet Daniel Ladinsky, come to mind:

> 'Ask anything,'
> My Lord said to me.
> And my mind and heart thought deeply
> for a second,
> then replied with just one word,
> 'When?'
> God's arms then opened up and I entered Myself.
> I entered Myself when I entered
> Christ.
> And having learned compassion I
> Allowed my soul
> to stay. [171]

The question 'When?' comes from a willingness to surrender, not only with the mind but also with a heartfelt response to the mystery of the Divine, trusting that the universe originates in infinite love and with faith in the goodness of Soul.

To return to St Thomas Aquinas, as I have come to understand, 'When?' means trusting that the response will be '*Now!*' The moment of asking requires a willingness to die in the sense of losing your life to find it. In the numinous rebirth that follows Lucid Surrender, 'death' can be met with gratitude, humility and joy, the more so as we learn through dreams how to develop such an attitude and to trust in the grace the Spirit within the dreams bestows.

While many Lucid Surrender encounters have taken me to other worlds of light, replete with life and learning, here, I will share just two dreams that were largely empty of form but nevertheless convey, in very direct and simple ways, the power and nature of surrender. In each dream, the unequivocal answer to 'When?' is unwaveringly 'Now!' Both dreams came during a period of painful and profound change in my life. Before each dream, I had spent time in contemplation and prayer, asking for guidance. In each features the presence of what I perceive as 'the Holy sands' of the Divine Ground.

Often in lucidity, after a transit on the Black Light or passage through a wormhole, there comes a stunning downward movement that slows as my invisible feet gently come to rest on an unseen surface of what feels like sand. In these sands, I feel all the stones, plants, animals and Beings of this sacred place rising in me, as though the source of Life itself is surging upwards through my soul. From this Ground of Being, visions of light and exaltation appear — numinous revelations of beauty, wonder, power, mystery and love.

The first dream that follows, which I have named 'Eternal Sands', felt like an invitation to delight in pure Absolute Being, but not before my mind was obliged to give up trying to make something happen!

With lucidity, the dreamscape and my dream body immediately fall away, and my soul is taken into the lucid space of Black Light and winds. 'I' remain a stationary point of consciousness on the sparkling blackness. Then, when I sing a prayer, my being feels carried at a tremendous speed across the Black Light at a great distance, as if I ride a magic carpet woven from the words and music of the prayer. I pass through filaments of white light against the shining black. After this comes another infinite expanse of vivid darkness. At some point, I think, 'What would you have me see, Lord?'

Eventually I find myself gently deposited face down onto a sand-covered expanse, surrounded by the Black Light. My subtle body now appears visible to me. This sandy space feels familiar from other lucid dreams in which I am usually set down feet first while awaiting whatever comes next. This time, I lie there moving my hands like rakes through the sands, aware of the raw silkiness of the sand between my fingers.

Apart from the dome of Black Light around me, I see nothing else beyond the rounded ring of sand. I notice that the sand looks similar in colour to the sand dunes of the Mojave Desert that I knew as a child on Earth – a warm, golden colour alight from within. I feel expectant, as the sands in lucid dreams generally set the stage for a memorable, numinous encounter. But this time 'nothing' appears.

My mind gets caught up in wondering about all this and what it might mean. But as I let the sand play through my fingers, I begin to feel in touch with both time and eternity, the hallmarks of the earthly and spiritual planes, as though an eternal hourglass cups my soul.

As my mind relaxes with the flow of the sand, I become aware of a strong, still Presence pervading the space. Even so, I ask, 'What would you have me do?', and I struggle to get up. With this, a powerful, magnetic force pulls me back down irresistibly and so I give in, thinking, 'Okay, I'll just rest here.'

I tuck my right hand under my head and finally surrender to the experience. It feels blissful to at last do nothing but finger the sand and the very fine, smooth, obsidian-like rocks that hide within it. Doing so assuages not only my own soul, but also the Spirit that I sense to be alive in these sands — elemental to all of existence.

After some time, my soul feels lovingly lifted and returned to waking consciousness. On the way, my mind kicks in again and tells me I ought to have done more, but the dream says, 'Rest in me.'

The second dream, which I have called 'Sand Angels', came a few weeks after the first. The dream echoes the theme of relinquishing the temporal *'When?'* for the eternal 'Now':

I wake up in the night and sing Psalm 51:10 to myself, 'Create in me a clean heart, Oh God, and renew a right spirit within me. Restore unto me the joy of Thy salvation and renew a right spirit within me.' Because I feel so weary, I ask for a dream of replenishment and for a sign that I am on the right path. Shortly after, I dream that I am walking by the sea. At first, I feel rather desultory, until I realise with joy that I am dreaming.

With lucidity, I again find myself on the Black Light as the dreamscape falls away. For a moment, I feel at a loss, but the winds rock me lovingly on the Black Light. They carry me on and on with incredible velocity. I feel too tired to pray or to worry, and so I simply submit.

Again, the winds place me belly down on the golden sands. This time. I extend my subtle arms out on either side and make the wings of sand angels. I feel grateful, happy to rest as I run my hands and arms through the sands. I try to rise but once more an unseen hand pushes me down between my shoulder blades. My face rests against the sands, and I give in to the delight of resting.

To my surprise, I am lifted and taken into an immense hall where I am whisked around and shown all its contents — a whimsical array of very fine and intricate imaginative figurines carved in a white translucent substance like ivory. I realise these figurines can come to life and that they have a connection to my own life on earth.

I feel inspired, as though I have been washed through with creative sparks. After being whirled around the hall, I am carried back across the Black Light and re-enter my body. I awaken feeling profoundly encouraged by the dream.

These dreams on 'the sands of Lucid Surrender' bring me to a new understanding of the sacred vision of Ibn al-'Arabi, who describes 'the sixth realm of the Sand Dune', a hill of white sand and musk that he calls a station before the 'Garden of Eden' wherein one finds the Presence and Qualities of the 'King' — the Divine.[172] The two dreams highlight that in Lucid Surrender the answer to the implicit question 'When?' is assuredly an explicit 'Now', as we are invited to find the miracle of life not in yesterday or tomorrow but in this heartbeat, this breath, this very moment in which God is born anew.

Notes:

169. Originally published in *Lucid Dreaming Experience*, 5, No. 2. (Sept. 2017): 26–29.
170. From 'Auguries of Innocence' in *The Pickering Manuscript* (http://www.kessinger.net: Kessinger Publishing), 15.
171. Ladinsky, *God's Love Poems*, 'Ask Anything', 131.
172. See Arabi's *Journey to the Lord of Power: A Sufi Manual on Retreat* (Rochester, Vermont: Inner Traditions International, 1989), 27, and Note No. 3 from 'The Commentary of 'Abdul-Karim Jili', 75–76.

Chapter 16

BECOMING AN ASTRONOMER OF DREAMS[173]

The cosmos is also within us.
We are made of star-stuff.
We are a way for the universe to know itself. [174]

— Carl Sagan

When we pause and look up in wonder at the night sky, we open ourselves to the blessing of gifts freely given and freely received. Entering our lucid dreams with open heart, we may likewise find ourselves infused with the spiritual presence of inner starlight, as happened to me in the following dream:

> *I feel very tired and in some pain from an inflamed disc in my spine but manage to say a few prayers before drifting off to sleep. With great gentleness and tenderness, my soul goes out of my dream body onto an infinite field of silky blackness.*
>
> *The Black Light has a delicate quality. A wind on the darkness arouses a sweet desire. Becoming lucid, I am aware of how much I need this and wonder what will happen next.*

The shimmering blackness opens to a stunning, azure blue that teems with clusters of stars — a beautiful tapestry of light. The blue appears both bright and deep as in a twilight sky strewn with countless stars. The constellations radiate life and intelligence. In contrast to the subtle vibrancy of the stars, I am aware of the denseness of my own life, the many responsibilities I carry and the weariness of my body, although I do not recall the factual details of my life.

I have the strong impression that every star has a connection to me and to waking life in some fundamental way — that each star longs for its light to be unveiled in the physical world. I feel humbly grateful for this revelation and for the beauty of the stars. With this awareness, my soul is again lifted gently onto the velvety black into wakefulness.

When I bring this spirit of gratitude to my dreams, I am led to a unified awareness of heart and mind, feelings and understanding, in Lucid Surrender.

Surrendering to gratitude, grace and praise in our dreams promotes wellbeing in waking life. Research has shown that if a depressed person simply writes down three things for which they feel thankful, even just once a week, then, after a few months, they will feel markedly better for it. [175] Imagine a world where everyone included 'dreams' on their list of what they feel thankful for! Yet people often discount their dreams, thereby losing out on the benefits dreams can bring.

Gratitude, considered to be one of the highest virtues, also requires humility to be received fully. Gratefulness and humility together open the heart to receive grace, developing our capacity to receive and, in turn, to give. Every dream, whether previously neglected, feared or tossed aside, has the potential to bring us psychological or spiritual benefit.

At the moment of lucidity, the dreamer often feels profoundly joyful and excited. Distracted by the intense emotion, many dreamers then pop out of lucidity. Instead, if the dreamer can become aware of a sense of thankfulness at the core of their joy and humbly express their gratitude towards the mysterious Presence suffusing the dream, this furthers the process of surrender. When lucid, I have found that focusing on giving thanks to the Divine helps to centre me. But in this next dream excerpt, gratitude spontaneously overcomes me:

Around 8.30 a.m. I wake up but feel so weary I decide to stay in bed. I attempt to say the Lord's Prayer but begin to fall back asleep. I hear a familiar whirring sound, a high, insistent pitch. Immediately, I feel that my soul is lifted onto the Black Light, something that hasn't happened for some time, and I feel deep joy and gratitude rise up through my weariness. I sense a chord of white laser light around my neck as waves of emotion rise up. Aware that the last time the chord appeared in a dream, I attempted to pull it away, this time I cry out in my thoughts, 'Yes! Whatever you want of me, Yes! Yes! Yes!'

Sometimes in Lucid Surrender, I find myself giving thanks to dream Beings who have carried me to a sacred space through wormholes or windswept space. For example, in the lucid dream that follows, an invisible Being carries me ever further into the inner reaches of a sacred space:

The unseen being gently sets me down on a great platform. I wonder if I stand on the edge of God's throne. My bare feet, shrouded in Black Light, feel awakened as they touch the soft and sacred ground. There, I am amazed to see a long eel-like beam of dark laser light move from my midriff, and I bow my head, saying, 'Thank you for bringing me here, Holy Being.'

As I wait in stillness, I am aware that my physical body is on the bed at home asleep, and I become afraid that my partner might inadvertently wake me up. This concerns me because if the lucid dream ends abruptly, I fear it may harm me. Then the unseen Presence says, 'You are safe.' As I take a step to turn towards the voice, the curious ground under my heels kicks up into a velvety jet-black cloud around me. The blackness feels richly full of light, with profound sweet Presence, and my consciousness now rests in this fullness and love.

I lose all sense of time until the black shining cloud recedes, and I know I must return home. Unsure of where my earthly 'home' is, I call out to the darkness, 'Please take me home now.' Again, my soul feels lifted onto winds across the Black Light. I am full of wonder at what has just happened and deeply grateful for the support of the unseen Being carrying me home.

Holy Beings often appear as light, but sometimes they may take on a more concrete form, as in this dream:

In the night, I awaken and sing. 'You my God are my heart's desire and my heart cries out to Thee…' The Spirit comes with a mighty whirring sound and lifts me onto the black, shining winds.

A definite but invisible Being cradles me in its arms and I am filled with ecstasy. After a while, we begin to descend, and I am curious about where I will be set down.

Rapidly we enter a hall so large I cannot see its end. What appear to be layers of flat, hard stones shaped like shale or slate in sheens of copper and black are interspersed with immense dark boulders, which spread over the hall's floor.

As we touch down, I take on a dream body and the Being becomes visible. He looks very slim or two-dimensional, with a long trapezoidal head and a featureless face that nevertheless communicates strongly felt Presence. His broad shoulders taper down into a triangle-tip waist. He has massive muscular arms and legs, a bit like a medieval knight wearing armour. I am so surprised by his unusual form that at first I feel disoriented. But then I remember he has been carrying me, and I say, 'Thank you, Holy Being, for bringing me here.' At this, he bows low from the waist towards me, revealing that he is only about half an inch thick, seemingly made of a substance similar to that covering the hall's floor. He looks as if he could easily be snapped apart, but I know the substance forming him is unbreakable. I feel taken aback that he should bow deferentially to me, but I manage to collect myself and bow in turn. After this, he walks away without speaking.

My eyes follow him, and I see a group of three or four magnificent celestial tigers with evident power and intelligence circling on a large boulder nearest to me. They walk so closely and smoothly together they look almost like flames swirling. Beyond the first cluster of tigers, I now see that on other boulders there appear similar clusters of tigers. The further I look, the more tigers materialise against the backdrop of vibrant darkness.

For a moment, I feel afraid that the tigers might leap down and devour me. Recalling the biblical story of 'Daniel in the Lion's Den', I realise that the tigers could easily overpower me if they chose to, so I decide to remain calm. The tigers remain focused on their circling, communicating a steady willpower and creative energy. I begin to sense that these tigers represent celestial Beings that have revealed themselves to me.

I wonder what the tigers will do and if they will speak or silently share with me their awesome beauty and concentrated power. Then the lucid dream comes to a sudden close, as the knight-like Being swoops me up and carries me back across the Black Light. How I would have liked to spend more time with the magnificent creatures!

It feels important and natural to give thanks to the Beings that help transport and care for me in the dreams. But beyond these encounters there is an intimately felt reciprocity with a more universal or transpersonal sense of Presence that dwells in the Holy spaces to which the Beings take me. In these encounters, the dream's purpose feels fully accomplished. Many such dreams have brought a profound infusion of vitality and love into my everyday life, as with the last dream to be included here:

I wake up in the night feeling despondent and lonely, and so I pray, repeating the Lord's Prayer. Eventually, curled up on my side, I drift off to sleep. Light forms begin to appear, and

I feel the lucid space open within me. Breathing out deeply through my mouth, I suddenly find myself moving on the Black Light through the opening between my lips. My invisible being abruptly falls 'headfirst' like a feather, spiralling down and down. I feel sad and lonely but then, realising I am not alone, I call out to the angels, 'Are you there?' In response, two Beings of swirling red light appear, turning like two hour-glasses of spiralling red light and accompanying me as I fall. Finally, we burst into an illuminated dark space, at the centre of which appears a solid black obsidian cylinder several feet across in diameter. Set down at its base, I observe that the black surface appears full of star-like pinpricks of light, and I think with great joy, 'The Divine?!'

I place my hands on either side of the cylindrical form peering into its mysterious beauty. With this, my soul is pulled into an infinite pool of star-laced blackness. Wondrous filaments of white light move through my soul. 'Oh, fill me!' I cry out, feeling immensely grateful and relieved.

After some time, I feel myself back in my dream body curled up on my side and peering closely at the cylinder again. As I look, dancing silver stars now spin to the left around its circumference. Kneeling again before the form, I place my hands on either side along the silver stars both to enhance and feel their spinning. 'Sweet silver angels!' I think to myself with wonder, feeling my hands alive with the spinning movement. The spinning creates a music to which the star Beings sing. I begin to sing joyfully too. Eventually, I awake with the hymn of praise on my lips, feeling I am meant to share this music in waking life through my words and actions.

We can think of our dreams in their manifold expression as visitations of light, shining out against the backdrop of the dark and sacred night. Origen, a Christian theologian of the 2nd century, was moved to say, 'Understand that you are a second little world and that the sun and the moon are within you, and also the stars.'[176] When we become astronomers of dreams, we see they are, like stars in the night sky, there to guide us.

NOTES:

173. Originally published in the *Lucid Dreaming Experience*, 7, No. 2 (September 2018): 18–24, as 'Stars in the Night Sky of Dreams'.
174. See Sagan's TV mini-series *Cosmos*, 'The Shores of the Cosmic Ocean', Season 1, Episode 1, 5:58–6:04, 28 September 1980, Director: Adrian Malone, Producer: Gregory Andorfer.
175. Robert A. Emmons and Michael E. McCullough, 'Counting Blessings Versus Burdens: An Experimental Investigation of Gratitude and Subjective Well-Being in Daily Life', *Journal of Personality and Social Psychology*, 84, No. 2 (2003): 377–389, doi: 10.1037/0022-3514.84.2.377
176. Jung, *The Collected Works*, Vol. 16, para 397.

Epilogue

In this vast Wheel of Creation wherein all things live and die,
wanders round the human soul like a swan in restless flying,
and she thinks that God is afar.
But when the love of God comes down upon her,
then she finds her own immortal life. [177]

— The Svetasvatara Upanishad

Like the swan in restless flight, I have travelled a good deal, living and working in many countries, looking for a place to make a 'home'. Finally, I settled on England, but not until I had first found the dwelling place of the soul in my own heart in Lucid Surrender.

At the level of Soul, our dreams work to make mystics of us all by re-orienting us towards God, who surpasses all definition but whom we may come to know as 'friend' and 'Beloved'. We need only to still the mind — whether awake or in dream sleep — to hear the voice of Love within, inspiring and renewing us each moment. Every dream offers an open invitation to know the thoughts of our heart and the guidance of Spirit.

My hope is that this collection of Lucid Surrender dreams will call to mind the healing power of Spirit, giving solace, wisdom and guidance, not least in the shadow of the Covid-19 pandemic.

As we seek ways to come through this time of upheaval, we need to learn how to live more in balance, both inwardly and outwardly with the natural world, as we remember the importance of simple pleasures, small kindnesses, warm gestures, and a more soulful way of life.

May our actions be rooted in the soil of the earth and nourished by our dreams. May we pursue the value of compassion as much as knowledge, as we discover how humanity and nature can flourish together. May dreams of Lucid Surrender encourage trust in the loving guidance of Spirit, as we choose how we shall yet live.

NOTES:

177. *The Upanishads,* translated and introduced by Juan Mascaro (Baltimore Maryland: Penguin Books, 1965), 85

Appendix: Guidance on the Path of Lucid Surrender

Qualities of the Lucid Dreamer that Facilitate Lucid Surrender

To varying degrees, the following characteristics are requisite for Lucid Surrender, but these qualities are then further developed and refined in dream lucidity — a process that is reciprocal:

- Mental and emotional balance.
- Awareness of a guiding Presence, Spirit, or quality to call on. (Over time, this becomes internalised).
- A deep yearning for Spirit and spiritual knowledge.
- Courage to take a leap into the unknown.
- Willingness to surrender to the irrational and paradoxical aspects of experience with curiosity and wonder.
- A heart-centered focus — activation of the intuitive mind.
- An attitude of humility, gratitude, reverence and praise.
- The acknowledgement of feelings and readiness to face what they may reveal.
- Patience to wait while "nothing" happens.
- The capacity to receive and contain both the light and the dark in the dream without fear or shame.

The Practice of Lucid Surrender

- Quietens the mind and opens the heart.
- Aligns consciousness and actions with a Higher Will.
- Provides guidance.

- Releases healing capacities within us.
- Imbues knowledge of the 'invisible' world.
- Inspires creative imagination.
- Dispels the illusion of separateness through the awareness of unitive consciousness.
- Heightens insight into situations and people.
- Enlarges our capacity to hold life's paradoxes with equanimity.
- Deepens our feeling capacity and sense of wonder.
- Affirms that we are both loved and capable of love.
- Reveals how the 'thinking' mind veils our soul nature.
- Fills, heals and renews us for waking life.

Preparing for Lucid Surrender
Waking-world activities that can be helpful:
- Be curious about dream lucidity.
- Be willing to use dreams to facilitate psychotherapeutic work, self-reflection and development for mental and emotional balance.
- Seek support in daily life from a spiritual community and/or a dream guide.
- Cultivate an attitude of prayerful gratitude for both the waking and dream worlds.
- Develop attentiveness and receptivity. Notice the extraordinary in the ordinary and the beauty of the everyday.
- Do bodywork to increase embodied awareness. This may be as simple as walking in Nature or a gentle yoga practice.
- Before falling asleep, still your mind and reaffirm your desire to remain present and aware in your dreams and to receive them openly. You can try mindfulness meditation,

prayer, or singing a sacred song. Use the breath to keep a steady, slow rhythm.

Become attentive in your dreams

The following examples are drawn from my own practice of cultivating a spirit of surrender in dream lucidity. You may find others:

- Become aware of time in the dream and how it relates to time in the waking life
- Pay attention to small objects in the dream, for example, stones, shells, feathers, sculptures or works of art. Pick them up and handle or touch them rather than passing them by.
- Observe closely colours or objects that look luminous, refined and clear and be especially attuned to beauty in a dream.
- Notice when the quality of the air is fluid or crystalline.
- Associate a colour or object with a given alchemical process (See Chapter Seven).
- Associate the dream landscape with an actual waking world landscape.
- Realise that threshold imagery such as a door, window or mirror can serve as a portal to a lucid experience
  (See Part III).
- Recognise that in your dream you may find yourself able to transcend the normal laws of physics; for example, you may be able to breathe underwater or fly, indicating that you have moved into a more subtle, lucid awareness.
- Try to identify a piece of music or art or read a text within the dream.

- Realise that you have been in a similar dream landscape or situation before.
- Enter into relationship with Dream Beings — ask their names, their intent, why they are present etc.
- Respond playfully to a person, thing, or situation that would otherwise frighten you in a dream and be curious about what may happen if you respond receptively.
- When invited or prompted to make love in a dream, remember the ultimate desire for union with the beloved aspect of the Divine in your soul.
- When undertaking an action in the dream, do so wholeheartedly with a 'Yes!' Sometimes, however, you need to trust your intuition and refuse when the invitation does not feel wholesome.
- Face and confront seemingly menacing dream characters, while maintaining awareness that fear in a dream indicates the presence of a defensive ego.
- Recognise a guide figure or guidance in a dream.

The Art of Surrender
- Enter the lucid dream with thankfulness and lightness of heart.
- Remain humble, devotional and respectful.
- Acknowledge any fear you may feel and move through it. Keep in mind that fear in a dream is often a construct of the mind. Treat fear as a challenge to develop courage in the face of the as-yet unknown.
- Try not to 'understand' what emerges in terms of normal waking world consciousness.

- Allow any imageless space simply to exist without imposing imagery.
- Begin meditating, drawing your attention to your breath and, if possible, repeating a mantra that you like to use in waking meditation.
- Have no expectations other than to be immersed in the experience.
- Seek guidance if you need it. You may find that the name of a divine or holy person comes to you spontaneously, or likewise a sacred song.
- Let go of any attempt to control the dream. Instead, be actively receptive.
- Let any action on your part arise spontaneously from a full, authentic response to the experience.
- Be prepared to 'let go' completely as you enter the lucid dream. You may experience your soul leaving your body. This may be accompanied by the sound of rushing wind and the feeling of being moved at hyper-speed through inner space.
- Recognise that while we can make ourselves ready for such experiences, we cannot make them happen just because it's what we want. We simply receive the gift as and when it comes.
- Remember that you always have the choice to remain in the lucid experience or to end it by coming out of the dream. (However, this may not be the case if you have taken a chemical substance to induce lucidity.)

Sustaining Lucid Surrender

Once you have entered a lucid dream, the following may help to maintain a lucid focus:

- If you find lucidity to be overwhelming, you may encounter what lucid dreamers call a 'false awakening'; that is, you may think you are awake while you are actually still in the dream state! This can be frightening if it seems you cannot get out of the dream at will. Yet, by dwelling on a sacred name or singing a sacred song, we become calm and from there we can choose whether or not to stay in the dream space.
- If you begin to lose focus in a lucid dream, you may find that abstract light-forms give way to more familiar form-based imagery. For instance if your concentration wanes, a sphere of light may change into a lamp, or you may find yourself in a brightly lit room. The ecstatic experience of cosmic union may transform into human lovemaking. Once you recognise what this signifies, the original lucid dream state is more likely to re-emerge.
- If the dream ends prematurely, don't berate yourself or mourn the loss. Simply prepare yourself to dream again!
- Recognise that if you find it too difficult to 'surrender' in a dream, you are now at least becoming conscious of the new dimensions that you are being invited to explore, and that further opportunities will come.

Returning to the Waking World

The following suggestions are intended to help retain the experience of a lucid dream and bring it into daily life — the aim being to live with greater lucidity in the waking world, as well as when you dream:

- Upon waking from a lucid dream — or any dream — take a few moments to lie still and to reflect on the dream before moving around.
- Take time to write down what you can recall of the dream, even if it's only a feeling, a colour or place.
- Resist the urge to judge yourself retrospectively or to feel disappointed if you have missed an opportunity to become lucid in a dream or were unable to stay lucid. Trust that dreams have their own rhythm and bring to light what can be safely received. In appreciating what has been missed, the grip of the ego loosens, as does the hold of the conditioned mind.
- Be aware that a lucid dream can bring greater awareness of unhelpful habits, patterns of thinking and behaviour that act as obstacles to knowledge of your soul nature.
- Some lucid dreams reveal how absurd our self-image and ways of thinking can be. Again, simply acknowledge this rather than condemning or judging yourself for it.
- Take time to review the life-context of the dream and how the dream might be speaking to you about your present circumstances and the choices before you.
- Reflect on how a dream may be correcting and compensating for a one-sidedness in your waking life. Consider what the dream suggests in support of your journey towards Individuation.

- Meditate on especially meaningful dream imagery.
- Give yourself time to rest and absorb the dream experience in the days that follow. A powerful lucid dream requires a great amount of psychic and physical energy and may take years to process fully! (Another reason why it is important to maintain a balanced and healthy lifestyle).
- Avoid becoming too attached to the idea of having an "experience" in a lucid dream or even to the prospect of achieving a lucid dream. Your dreams provide a landscape for the journey you are making, but the destination is in the gift of your soul.
- Lucid dreams can be self-revelatory and complete in themselves. However, working with a dream guide may help bring 'unfinished' dreams to fulfilment, taking you more deeply into Lucid Surrender.

Bibliography

Adler, G., and McGuire, W. (eds) *The Collected Works of C. G. Jung*, trans. R. F. C. Hull, Herbert Read, Michael Fordham (London: Routledge & Kegan Paul, various dates)

Adler, Gerhard. (ed.) *C. G. Jung's Letters: Volume 2, 1951–1961*, in collaboration with Aniela Jaffé, trans. R. F. C Hull (London: Routledge & Kegan Paul, 1976)

Aftel, Maggie, *The Essence of Alchemy: A Book of Perfume* (New York, NY: North Point Press, 1991)

al-Jilani, Hadrat Abd al-Qadir. *The Secret of Secrets*, trans. Shaykh Tosun Bayrak al-Jerrahi al-Halveti (The Islamic Text Society: Cambridge, 1991)

Arabi, Ibn. *Journey to the Lord of Power: A Sufi Manual on Retreat* (Rochester, Vermont: Inner Traditions International, 1989)

Arabi, Ibn. *The Bezels of Wisdom* (Classics of Western Spirituality), trans. R. W. J. Austin (Mahwah, New Jersey: Paulist Press, Inc., 1980)

Assagioli, Roberto. *The Act of Will* (New York, NY: Penguin Group, 1973)

de Avila, Teresa. *Interior Castle: The Classic Text with Spiritual Commentary*, C.Ss.R (Notre Dame, Indiana: Ave Marie Press, Inc,. 2007)

de Avila, Teresa. *Love Poems from God: Twelve Sacred Voices from the East and West*, trans. Daniel Ladinsky (Penguin Group: New York, 2006)

Azriel of Gerona, Rabbi. *Meditation and Kabbalah*, trans. Aryeh Kaplan (Lanham, Maryland: Rowman & Littlefield, Inc., 1995)

Blake, William, 'Auguries of Innocence', *The Pickering Manuscript*. (Whitefish, Montana: Kessinger Publishers, LLC, 2010).

Bogzaran, Fariba. 'Hyperspace Lucidity and Creative Consciousness', in Kelly Bulkeley and Ryan Hurd (eds), *Lucid Dreaming: New Perspectives on Consciousness in Sleep*, Vol. 2 (Santa Barbara, CA: Praeger, 2014), 209-231

Bourgeault, Cynthia. *Centering Prayer and Inner Awakening* (Cambridge, Massachusetts: Cowley Publishing, 2004)

Bulkeley, Kelly. *Dreaming in the World's Religions: A Comparative History* (New York, NY: New York University Press, 2008)

Chevalier, J., and Gheerbrant, A. *The Penguin Dictionary of Symbols*, trans. John Buchanan-Brown (London: Penguin Books, 1996)

Chittick, William C. *Imaginal Worlds: Ibn al-'Arabi and the Problem of Religious Diversity* (Albany, New York: Suny Press, 1994)

Commentaria in Scripturam Sacram, Paris 1878, vol. 9, 541. Tradition in Action:https://www.traditioninaction.org/religious/n002rp Lapide_Appearance.htm

Corbin, Henry. *Alone with the Alone: Creative Imagination in the Sufism of Ibn Arabi*, trans. Willard Trask (Princeton: Princeton University Press, 1969)

Corbin, Henry. *Swedenborg and Esoteric Islam: Comparative Spiritual Hermeneutics*, trans. Leonard Fox (West Chester, PA: Swedenborg Studies, 1995)

Corbin, Henry. *The Man of Light in Iranian Sufism* (Omega Publications: New Lebanon, New York, 1994)

Crayon Angel: A Tribute to the Music of Judee Sill, American Dust, 1971, compact disc.

David ben Yehuda he Hasid, R. *Book of Mirrors: Sefer 'Mar ot ha-Zove' ot*, ed. by Daniel Chanad Matt (Chico, California: Scholar Press, 1982)

de Nicolás, Antonio T. (trans. and with commentary by) *St John of the Cross (San Juan de la Cruz): Alchemist of the Soul: His Life, His Poetry, His Prose* (York Beach, Maine: Samuel Weisser, Inc., 1989) de Pascalis, Andrea. *Alchemy the Golden Art: The Secrets of the Oldest Enigma* (Gremese International: Rome, 1995)

de Rola, Stanislas Klossowski. *Alchemy: The Secret Art* (London: Thames & Hudson Ltd., 1973, 1997)

Delahaye, Elisabeth. *The Lady and the Unicorn* (Paris: Editions de la Réunion de Musées Nationaux, 2007)

Edinger, Edward F. *The New God Image: A Study of Jung's Key Letters Concerning the Evolution of the Western God-Image*, eds. D. D. Cordic and C. Yates (Wilmette, IL: Chiron Publications, 1996)

Edinger, Edward. *The Mystery of the Coniunctio: Alchemical Image of Individuation* (Toronto, Canada: Inner City Books, 1994)

Emmons, R. A. and McCullough, M. E. 'Counting Blessings Versus Burdens: An Experimental Investigation of Gratitude and Subjective Well-Being in Daily Life', *Journal of Personality and Social Psychology*, 84, No. 2 (2003): 377–389, doi: 10.1037/0022-3514.84.2.377

Esser, Ted. 'Kundalini and Non-Duality in the Lucid Dreaming State', in Kelly Bulkeley and Ryan Hurd (eds), *Lucid Dreaming: New Perspectives on Consciousness in Sleep*, Vol. 2 (Santa Barbara, CA: Praeger, 2014), 233–263

Faiman, James, and Frager, Robert (eds). *Essential Sufism* (San Francisco, California: Harper Collings Publishers, 1997)

Feng, G-F., and English, J. (trans.) *Chuang Tsu Inner Chapters: A Companion Volume to the Tao Te Ching* (San Francisco, California: Amber Lotus Publishing, 2000)

Fenwick, P. and Fenwick, E. *The Truth in the Light: An Investigation of over 300 Near-Death Experiences* (London: Headline Book Publishing, 1995)

Feynman, Richard P. *The Strange Theory of Light and Matter* (Great Britain: Penguin Books, 1990)

Forshaw, Peter J. '"Behold, the dream cometh": Hyperphysical Magic and Deific Visions in an Early-Modern Theosophical Lab-Oratory', in *Conversations with Angels: Essays Towards a History of Spiritual Communication, 1100–1700*, ed. Joad Raymond, 175–200 (UK: Palgrave, Macmillan, 2011)

Garfield, Patricia. *Pathways to Ecstasy: The Way of the Dream Mandala* (New York, NY: Prentice Hall Press, 1979)

Gibran, Khalil. *The Prophet* (New York, NY: Alfred A. Knopf, 1951)

Gillespie, George. 'Light and Lucid Dreams: A Review', in *Dreaming*, 2, No. 3 (1992): 167–179

Gillespie, George. *Seeing: Beyond Dreaming to Religious Experiences of Light* (Exeter, UK: Imprint Academic, 2019)

Gittings, Robert. (ed.) *The Letters of John Keats* (Oxford: Oxford University Press, 1970, 1982)

Gregory, Richard L. 'Shaving in a Mirror with Ockham's Razor', in Miranda Anderson (ed.), *An Interdisciplinary Collection Exploring the Cultural Story of the Mirror* (Newcastle: Cambridge Scholars Publishing, 2008), 94–104

Grof, Stanislov, *Beyond the Brain: Birth, Death, and Transcendence in Psychotherapy*, Suny Series in Transpersonal and Humanistic Psychology, eds. Richard D. Mann and Jeanne B. Mann (Albany: State University of New York, 1985)

Hafiz. 'My Brilliant Image', from *I Heard God Laughing: Poems of Hope and Joy: Renderings of Hafiz*, trans. Daniel Ladinsky (London: Penguin Books Ltd., 2006)

Hagelin, John. 'Entanglement, Space-Time Wormholes, and the Brain', *Science and Nonduality Series*, 5 December 2014, https://www.youtube.com/watch?v=nvVDYQoGWyk

Hamilton, Nigel. 'Dreams of Awakening' (IASD Conference presentation, Berkeley, 2012)

Hamilton, Nigel. 'Psychospiritual Transformation: Light, Colour, and Symmetry', in Robert J. Hoss and Robert P. Gongloff (eds), *Dreams: Understanding Biology, Psychology, and Culture*, Vol. 2 (Santa Barbara, CA: ABC-CLIO, LLC, 2019), 634–640

Hamilton, Nigel. *Awakening Through Dreams: The Journey Through the Inner Landscape* (London: Karnac Books, 2014)

Henderson, J. L. and Sherwood, D. N. *Transformation of the Psyche: The Symbolic Alchemy of the Slendor Solis* (London and New York: Routledge Taylor & Francis Group, 2005)

Hillman, James. *Re-Visioning Psychology* (NewYork, NY: Harper Collins, 1975)

Hirtenstein, Stephen. 'Muhyiddin Ibn 'Arabi: The Treasure of Compassion', passage 1.59 from the *Futuhat*, trans. William Chittick in *Beshara*, No. 12 (Autumn/Winter 1990): 30–38, http://beshara-magazine.org/wp-content/uploads/2016/10/Issue-12-clear.pdf

Hobson, J. Allan. 'The Neurobiology of Consciousness: Lucid Dreaming Wakes Up', *The International Journal of Dream Research*, 2, No. 2 (October 2009): 41–44

Hurd, Ryan. 'Spontaneous Emergence: A Phenomenology of Lucid Dreaming' (Master's thesis, R. D. Hurd, 2008), http://www.driccpe.org.uk/?s=hurd

Jaffé, Aniela (ed.) *C.G. Jung: Word and Image*, Bollingen Series XCVII, Vol. 2 (Princeton, NJ: Princeton University Press, 1979)

Jarrett, James L. (ed.), *C. G. Jung: The Seminars, Nietzsche's Zarathustra: Notes on the Seminar Given in 1934–39* by C. G. Jung, Vol. 2, Part I, 13 March 1935 (New York, NY: Routledge, 1989)

Johnson, Robert. *Inner Gold: Understanding Psychological Projection* (Kilhei Hawaii: Koa Books, 2008)

Jung, Carl. *Aion* (Princeton: Princeton University Press, 2nd edition, 1969)

Jung, Carl. *Memories, Dreams, Reflections*, ed. Aniela Jaffé, trans. Richard and Clara Winston (New York: Random House, 1965)

Jung, Carl. *The Undiscovered Self*, 4th edition, trans. R. F. C. Hull (London: Routledge & Kegan Paul, 1958, 1969)

Kellogg, E. and Ziemer, Mary [Powell, Melinda]. 'Lucid Dream Alchemy: The Making of the Philosopher's Stone', presented at the International Association for the Study of Dreams Psiber Dreaming Conference, 2014, https://www.academia.edu/18468306/Lucid_Dream_Alchemy_Making_the_Philosophers_Stone

Kelsey, Morton T. *God, Dreams, and Revelations: A Christian Interpretation of Dreams* (Minneapolis, MI: Augsburg Fortress Publishing, 1991)

Khan, Pir Vilayat Inayat. *Introducing Spirituality into Counselling and Therapy* (New Lebanon, NY: Omega Publications, 1969, 1982)

La Berge, Stephen, Nagel, Lynn, Dement, William C., Zarcone Jr., Vincent. 'Lucid Dreaming Verified by Volitional Communication During REM Sleep', *Perceptual and Motor Skills*, 52 (1981): 727–732

LaBerge, Stephen. *Lucid Dreaming* (New York, NY: Tarcher, 1985)

Lao Tzu, *Tao Te Ching*, trans. Stephen Mitchell (New York, NY: Harper Perennial Modern Classics, 2006)

Maier, Michael. *Atalanta Fugiens: Sources of an Alchemical Book of Emblems*, ed. H. M. E. De Jong (York Beach, ME: Nicolas-Hays Inc., 2002)

Marlan, Stanton. *The Black Sun: The Alchemy and Art of Darkness* (Texas: A & M University Press, 2005)

McLean, Adam. *The Alchemical Mandala: A Survey of the Mandala in the Western Esoteric Tradition* (Grand Rapids, MI: Phanes Press, 2002)

Misner, Charles W. and Wheeler, John A. 'Classical physics as geometry', *Annals of Physics*, 2, No. 6 (1957): 525, doi:10.1016/0003-4916(57)90049-0

Modesto, R., and Mount, G. *Not for Innocent Ears: Traditions of a Desert Cahuilla Medicine Woman* (Sweetlight Books, 1986)

Mookerjee, Ajit. *Kali: The Feminine Force* (London: Thames & Hudson, Ltd., 1988)

Moss, Robert. *The Secret History of Dreams* (Novato, California: New World Library, 2009)

NASA, 'Dark Energy, Dark Matter', accessed 10 July 2020, https://science.nasa.gov/astrophysics/focus-areas/what-is-dark-energy

Nasr, Sayyed Hossein. *The Garden of Truth: The Vision and Promise of Sufism, Islam's Mystical Tradition* (New York, NY: Harper One, 2007)

Nrobu, Choygal Namkhai. *Dream Yoga and the Practice of Natural Light* (Ithaca, NY: Snow Lion Publications, 1992)

Obousy, R. K. and Cleaver, G. 'Putting the "Warp" Back into Warp Drive', *Spaceflight*, 50, No. 4 (April 2008): Figure 2, arXiv:0807.1957v2 [physics.pop-ph]

Pagel, James F. 'The Synchronous Electrophysiology of Conscious States', *Dreaming*, 22, No. 3 (2012): 179, doi: 10.1037/a0029659

Paracelsus, *Selected Writings*, Bollingen Series XXVIII, ed. Jolande Jacobi, trans. Norbert Guterman (Princeton, NJ: Princeton University Press, 1988)

Powell, Andrew. *The Ways of the Soul: A Psychiatrist Reflects, Essays on Life, Death and Beyond* (London: Muswell Hill Press, 2017)

Powell, Melinda, *The Hidden Lives of Dreams* (Bonnier Books, 2020).

Prins, Jacomien. 'Mirrors as Transmitters of Divine Harmony', in Miranda Anderson, *An Interdisciplinary Collection Exploring the Cultural Story of the Mirror* (Newcastle: Cambridge Scholars Publishing, 2008), 80–91

Rilke, Rainer Maria. *Das Stunden Buch* (Berlin, Germany: Insel Verlag, 1996)

Rilke, Rainer Maria. *Rilke's Book of Hours: Love Poems from God*, trans. Anita Barrows and Joanna Macy (New York: Riverhead Books, 1996)

Ripley, Sir George. *Compound of Alchymie* in *Ripley Reviv'd*, Eirenaeus Philalethes (William Cooper), Early English Books Online Text Creation Partnership, 2011, https://quod.lib.umich.edu/e/eebo/A61326.0001.001/1:13.5?rgn=div2;view=fulltext

Roob, Alexander. *The Hermetic Museum: Alchemy & Mysticism* (Köln: TASCHEN GmbH, 2006)

Rowling, J. K., *Harry Potter and the Philosopher's Stone* (London: Bloomsbury Publisher's, 1997)

Sagan, Carl. 'The Shores of the Cosmic Ocean', *Cosmos*, Season 1, Episode 1, 5:58–6:04, 28 September 1980, Director: Adrian Malone, Producer: Gregory Andorfer

Schädlich, Michael and Erlacher, Daniel. 'Lucid Music — A Pilot Study Exploring Experiences and Potentials of Music-Making in Lucid Dreams', *Dreaming*, 28, No. 3 (September 2018): 276–286, doi: 10.1037drm0000073

Scholem, Gershom. *Kabbalah* (New York, NY: Meridian, 1978)

Sendivogius, Michael. *The New Chemical Light. Second part. Concerning Sulphur*, ed. Jean Pierre Donabin (originally published by J. Elliot and Co., London, 1893), http://www.livres-d-hermes.com/PDF/NEWCH101.PDF

Shabistari, Mahmud. *The Garden of Mystery*, trans. Robert Abdul Hayy Darr (Cambridge: Cherwynd House, 2007)

Shainberg, Catherine. *Kabbalah and the Power of Dreaming: Awakening the Visionary Life* (Rochester, NY: Inner Traditions, 2005)

Sheldrake, Rupert. *Science and Spiritual Practices: Reconnecting Through Direct Experience* (London: Coronet, 2017)

Sparrow, Scott. *Lucid Dreaming: Dawning of the Clear Light* (Virginia Beach, VA: Edgar Cayce Foundation, 1976)

Steele, Robert and Waley Singer, Dorothea. 'The Emerald Table', *Proceedings of the Royal Society of Medicine*, 21, No. 3 (January 1928): 485–501, https://www.ncbi.nlm.nih.gov/pmc/articles/PC2101974/?page=1

Stumbrys, Tadas, Erlacher, Daniel, and Schredl, Michael. 'Effectiveness of Motor Practice in Lucid Dreams: a Comparison with Physical and Mental Practice', *Journal of Sports Sciences* (2015) http://www.tandfonline.com/doi/abs/10.1080/02640414.2015.1030342

Synesisus of Cyrene. *On Dreams*, ed. and trans. Augustine Fitzgerald, The Essays and Hymns of Synesius of Cyrene, Vols. 1–2 (Oxford: Oxford University Press, 1930)

Szulakowska, Urszula. *The Alchemy of Light: Geometry and Optics in Late Renaissance Alchemical Illustration* (Boston, Massachusetts: Brill, 2000)

The Chymical Wedding of Christian Rosenkreutz (1616): Acrobat edition prepared by Benjamin Rowe, October 2000: https://39514839f4a6d-c8a84ae-eaa972a576b84b28f1b3596cd9812f8f.ssl.cf5.rackcdn.com/chymical_wedding.pdf

The Oxford Classical Dictionary (Oxford: Oxford University Press, 2012)

The Upanishads, translated and introduced by Juan Mascaro (Baltimore, Maryland: Penguin Books, 1965)

Thorne, Kip S. *Black Holes & Time Warps: Einstein's Outrageous Legacy* (New York and London: W. W. Norton & Company, 1994)

Tyler, Peter. *Teresa of Avila: Doctor of the Soul* (London, UK: Bloomsbury Publishing, Plc., 2013)

Uyl, Anthony. (ed.) *The Collected Works of Dionysius the Aeropagite*, trans. Rev. John Parker (Ontario, Canada: Solace Games, 2015)

Vandenbos, G. R. (ed.) *The APA Dictionary of Psychology* (Washington, D.C.: American Psychological Association, Washington DC, 2007)

Villaseñor, David. *Tapestries in Sand: The Spirit of Indian Sand Painting* (Happy Camp, California: Naturegraph Company Publishers, Inc., 1966)

Voss, Ursula and Hobson, Allan. 'What is the State-of-the-Art on Lucid Dreaming? – Recent Advances and Further Questions', *Open MIND*, eds. Thomas Metzinger and Jennifer M. Windt (Frankfurt am Main: MIND Group, 2015): 4, doi: 10.15502/9783958570306

Voss, Ursula et al. 'Lucid Dreaming: A State of Consciousness with Features of Both Waking and Non-Lucid Dreaming', *Sleep*, 32, No. 9 (1 September 2009): 1191–1200, https://www.ncbi.nlm.nih.gov/pmc/articles/PMC2737577/

Voss, Ursula. 'The Healing Sands of Lucid Dreamtime', *Lucid Dream Exchange*, No. 58 (March 2011): 12–16

Waggoner, Robert. 'A Dreamspeak Interview with Robert Waggoner', *Lucid Dreaming Experience*, 1, No. 4 (March 2013): 2–12

Waggoner, Robert. *Lucid Dreaming Gateway to the Inner Self* (Moment Point Press: 2009)

Wangyal, Tenzin Rinpoche. *Awakening the Luminous Mind: Tibetan Meditation for Inner Peace and Joy*, ed. Marcy Vaughn (London: Hay House, Inc., 2012)

Whitmont, E. C. and Brinton Perera, S. *Dreams: A Portal to the Source* (London: Brunner-Routledge, 1989, 1994)

Winnicott, D.W. 'Mirror-role of Mother and Family in Child Development', in *Playing and Reality* (London and New York: Routledge Classics edition, 1971, 2005), 149–159

Yeats, W. B. *William Butler Yeats: Selected Poems and Three Plays*, 4th edition, ed. M. L. Rosenthal (New York, NY: Scribner Paperback Poetry Edition, Simon & Schuster, Inc., 1996)

Zajonc, Arthur. *Catching the Light: The Entwined History of Light and Mind* (New York and Oxford: Oxford University Press, 1993)

Ziemer, Mary [Powell, Melinda]. 'Stars in the Night Sky of Dreams', *Lucid Dreaming Experience*, 7, No. 2 (September 2018): 18–24

Ziemer, Mary [Powell, Melinda]. 'Love's Lucid Labours Nearly Lost', in *Lucid Dreaming Experience*, 2, No. 4 (March 2014): 13–15

Ziemer, Mary [Powell, Melinda]. 'Lucid Surrender and the Holy Tree', *Lucid Dreaming Experience*, 2, No. 3, December 2013, 8–9

Ziemer, Mary [Powell, Melinda]. 'Lucid Surrender and Jung's Alchemical *Coniunctio*' in *Lucid Dreaming: New Perspectives on Consciousness in Sleep*, Vol. 1, eds. Ryan Hurd and Kelly Bulkeley (Santa Barbara, CA: Praeger, 2014), 145–166

Ziemer, Mary [Powell, Melinda]. 'Beyond the Matrix: From Consensus Reality to Heart Consciousness', *Lucid Dreaming Experience*, 2, No. 1 (June 2013): 20–27

Ziemer, Mary [Powell, Melinda]. 'Through a Glass Lucidly', in *Lucid Dreaming Experience*, 2, No. 2 (September 2013): 9–15

Ziemer, Mary [Powell, Melinda]. 'Lucid Surrender and the Alchemical *Coniunctio*', *Lucid Dreaming: New Perspectives on Consciousness in Sleep*, Vol. 2, eds. Kelly Bulkeley and Ryan Hurd (Santa Barbara, California: Praeger, 2014), 145–166

Ziemer, Mary [Powell, Melinda]. 'The Sacred Sands of Lucid Surrender', *Lucid Dreaming Experience*, 5, No. 2. (Sept. 2017): 26–29

Ziemer, Mary [Powell, Melinda].'The Alchemy and Archetype of Black Light in Lucid Surrender', *DreamTime Magazine* (March 2012)

About The Author

Inspired by her dreams, Melinda Powell co-founded the Dream Institute, at the Centre for Counselling and Psychotherapy Education, London, to promote research into the relationship between dreams and wellbeing. Melinda has served as past vice-president of the International Association for the Study of Dreams and as director of Help Counselling Centre. She works as a psychotherapist and teaches the art of Lucid Dreaming. Melinda has published and lectured widely on dreams and lucidity. Born in Southern California, she lived for a number of years in Poland and Switzerland before making her home in the United Kingdom.

Melinda Powell approaches lucid dreaming as a means to soul-awakening, a path she calls 'Lucid Surrender'™. This book derives from Powell's firsthand experience as a lucid dreamer, her professional work as a psychotherapist and her researches into lucid dreaming. Her application of Carl Jung's alchemical model to Lucid Surrender brings new dimensions to our understanding of alchemy, therapeutic practice and dream lucidity. She describes how stages similar to the alchemical process can also be *consciously* initiated in a lucid dream, with powerful therapeutic effect. Powell further develops Jung's teachings on light, revisioning the reader's understanding of darkness by illuminating the phenomenon of Black Light. She shows how lucid dreams can open us to the realm of the transpersonal.

Text Credits

'Every Prophet's Name' and 'Ask Anything' from the Penguin publication *Love Poems From God: Twelve Sacred Voices East and West* by Daniel Ladinsky, copyright 2002, and used with permission.

'My Brilliant Image' from the Penguin publication *I Heard God Laughing: Poems of Hope and Joy: Renderings of Hafiz* by Daniel Ladinsky, copyright 1996 and 2006, and used with permission.